Bernadette's Book

HUGH ORAM

www.trafford.com

North America & international
toll-free: 1 888 232 4444 (USA & Canada)
phone: 250 383 6864 ♦ fax: 812 355 4082

Contents

Bernadette's Poems, Published and Unpublished

Bernadette's life story

Bernadette's Poems, Published and Unpublished

Bernadette as a young woman; she would have been
in her early 20s when this photograph was taken.

The Hour

1

We stood upon the pavement cold and grey
The Céilide o' er this was the parting hour
Within your arms my spirit soared away
Ascending to the hills wherein a bower

2

Fashioned by nature lies a magic place
Carpeted with sea—green moss and above
A canopy of pine trees interlace
Diana draped her mantle o' er our love

3

The sky a patch of velvet deep and blue
The moon a pearl all lustrous and bright
The heavens star—sequestered and with you
My being merged in celestial light

4

The nectar of the Gods was mine the joy
They knew in spheres Elysian the same
That once consumed proud Paris prince of Troy
And queenly Helen in its passion flame
I was as Grainne fair who once had fled
With Diarmuid to fulfill a love as doomed
To tragic end on Bulben' s craggy head
As hers did then my hopes lie entombed

5

A happiness like theirs was mine for one brief hour
Until relucant from your arms I crept
I saw my shattered hopes fall in a shower
Of rainbow fragment, in my heart I wept

6

The cool clear winds of reason brushed my face
As dawn approached on tip—toe o' er the sky
Vanished the bower of bliss the magic place
We stood upon the pavement you and I

Published, Ireland' s Own, April 21,1951

4

Abandonment

1

Steeped in moonlight the mountain road wound,
Curling in loops fantastic and gay
A strip of silver—splashed ribbon bound
Around nature's verdant tresses lay

2

Together we went with wanton glee
Heady with gorse and heather perfume
Pilfered and borne on winds of the shee
Their fragrance upon our pathway strewn

3

Pine Forest and ethereal wood
Wrapped in a mantle of silver green
Hellfire a smbre sentinel stood
Eerily etched in a pale moonbeam

4

We heard the harpers play in the wind,
Their faery music our souls entranced
And seeking our hearts' desire to find
With a wild abandoned glee we danced

5

No longer mortal beings were we
With eyes agleam and with lips apart
At one with the ever lasting shee
With the ageless ones the young at heart

6

Exultant beauty everywhere tripped
A mocking ever elusive wraith
That flitted on moonwashed heights bronze—tipped
O' er snowy summits to where beneath

7

Like a myriad of floating stars
In the mighty cauldron of the night
There hung suspended on golden bar
From the moon the city all alight

8

Longing with you this moment to share
Within my heart I echoed your name
The pretence was o' er you were no there
Alone with a dream I longed in vain

Escape

1

O life thou stark reality
To me it seems
If I could but escape from thee
To where my dreams
Might be fulfilled
I could be happy

2

There I would find my heart's content
In this release
My soul no longer earthwards bent
Would be at peace
It could rejoice
I would be happy

3

The hopes and fears of restless youth
Would pass away
My ideal in this land of truth
With me would stay
What joyous thought
To be so happy

4

If only an escape like this
My soul set free
To realms of ecstatic bliss
Thus would I flee
My dreams fulfill
And so be happy

Dream House

1

At the foot of yon blue mountains
I would build my house of dreams
In the glen where faery fountains
Cascade into silver streams

2

White washed walls with windows shining
'Neath a golden thatch so neat
Round the door red roses twining
From the eaves a bird song sweet

3

Trees of bright red rowan nodding
Near a door of apple green
King Sol' s golden fingers prodding
Russet branches all agleam

4

All around them in confusion
Strewn in colourful array
Blossoms bloom in sweet profusion
Stars upon the Milky Way

5
Deep suffusing colour glowing
Midst these fragile fragrant flowers
Heather perfumed breezes blowing
From the hills in scented showers

6
Soul—subduing silence ever
In this magic woodland glade
In my shieling midst the heather
'Neath the tall pines sombre shade

Published Ireland' s Own, February 24, 1951; Rosc, June—July, 1953; Cork Weekly Examiner

Before and After

1

Grey galleons of gilded cloud
In grandeur swept across the sky
Pursued by winds that crying loud
Proclaimed their monarchy on high

2

These pirate ships with cargoes bright
Sought vainly to elude pursuit
The sky became as black as night
As seeking to return their loot

3

By howling winds were rent in twain
Spilling their shining contents down
To drench the earth in sparkling rain
Like silver spears from Heaven thrown

4

From midst the wreckage wrought on high
By these same winds that
March doth bring
With rainbow retinue drawn nigh
To lay him court there came a king

5

Clad regally in raiment bright
A golden crown upon his head
From which shot slanting rays of light
Subdued the wicked winds now fled

6

Translucent tapestry of Spring
Bestrewn with silver raindrops lay
Upon the earth, the birds did sing
With joy. All clouds must pass away

Evening

1

Way up among the hills so blue
A vision once I did behold
Arrayed in robes of varied blue
Her tresses of the brightest gold

2

In artist' s guise across the sky
With pastel shades she lightly tipped
Each gilt—edged cloud as she passed by
Her brush in magic dew she dipped

3

With colours delicate and rare
She painted o' er the Milky Way
And almost hidden in her hair
Lingered the last faint rays of May

4

The mountain peaks were all ablaze
With splendour as she o' er them shed
Her mantle of shimmering haze
Then on towards the West she sped

5

Still in her artist guise arrayed
Over the sea each dancing wave
With powdery colours lightly sprayed
As they to her their homage gave

6

The vision faded from my sight
And in her place I saw on high
Out of the East the spirit of night
Approaching swiftly o' er the sky

Published, Rosc, January—February, 1951; Cork Weekly Examiner

Autumnal Winds

1

The leaves are tossed into the air
Pale petals everywhere are strewn
Autumn tossing the burnished hair
Dances beneath the waning moon

2

In swirling gusts on land and sea
The winnowing winds wildly sigh
A moaning mournful melody
Sombre symphony sweeps the sky

3

While trailing scarves of mist that curl
Round leafless branches brown and haze
In whirling eddies break and hurl
Like cymbal clashes cleave the air

4

Rustling russet leaves now shed
Twirling through the trembling trees
Sighing for summer splendours sped
Like wreaths of vapour in the breeze

5

Sullen clouds before them race
Across the stricken sky they flee
Swollen streams now turbulent chase
In rushing torrents to the sea

6

The dying year now nears a close
Weird whining winds her dirges sing
Nature nestling in repose
Awaits the promised birth of spring

Interlude

1

Entranced my way I wended
Through a floral faeryland
Where delicate tints are blended
By a fragile faery hand

2

I beheld the wee folk peeping
From the heart of every flower
Out of which they come a leaping
At the moon's bewitching hour

3

Their jewel—crusted mantles shimmered
Merged in incandescent light
Diamond dew—drops gaily glimmered
On gossamer garments bright

4

Naïve nymphs nimbly neatly flinging
Cloaks from curving petals made
Over slender sylph spirits singing
Sad sweet songs 'neath sylvan shade

5

Gold crowned lilies white entrancing
Gently whispered with the breeze
Piquant playmate proudly dancing
Tripped and treaded through the trees

6

Reluctant my way I wended
From this magic perfumed glade
Deep suffused in colour blended
Where the faery fountains played

Published, Cork Weekly Examiner

Passing Wishes

1

Neath yon mountains shelter set me
When life's toils and cares are o'er
In a bed of heather let me
Sleep in peace for ever more

2

Sleep in slumber deep unending
Yes I will and this I'll find
Sweet contentment ever blending
Peace to quell a restless mind

3

O'er the place where I am
Mountain pines lying a watch will keep
Softly in the night winds sighing
Sleep perturbed spirit sleep

4

All of life's vain care and sorrow
Shall assail my soul no more
Mine shall be a glad tomorrow
On the all eternal shore

A Shower

1

Jewel—laden clouds of sapphire sped
Like chariots across the sky
O' er reawakened earth they shed
Cascading showers from on high

2

Sparkling showers from silver spun
From out the sky came tumbling down
In pearl—like drops that every one
Cling fast to nature' s floral gown

3

Like myriads of stars they lay
Upon the earth' s green garment bright
O' er trees in glittering array
Surrounded by translucent light

4

Receding clouds behind them flung
A mantle bright of rainbow hue
From which with golden splendour sprung
Phoebus triumphant into view

5

Exultant from within its fold
He dropped on every flower a kiss
Their petals silver shot with gold
Trembled in ecstatic bliss

6

Thus softly as this shower passed
Its fading fragile fragrance fell
Caressed with cloak o' er Nature cast
Beneath the magic of its spell

Published, Ireland' s Own, August 7, 1951; Cork Weekly Examiner (no date given)

Nightfall in Tyrol

1
Like a bird of prey
Swiftly silently
In alpine regions
Descended the night
And the frightened day
Quickly quietly
By hostile legions
Encompassed took flight

2
Like a dying swan
Gliding gracefully
Over the mountains
Her life's red blood
From her wounded breast
Spilling suddenly
In spurting fountains
Like a crimson flood

3
The snow powdered peaks
Softly shimmering
Suffused in colours
Flamboyant and gay

Reflected the streaks
Burning brilliantly
The sky now darkened
By the passing day

4
She sang the last song
Moaning mournfully
Her frail voice blending
With breezes of night
And they piped her dirge
Singing sombrely
Her brief life ending
She faded from light

Published, Cork Weekly Examiner, January 5, 1952

In the distance

1

Enchanted city of my dreams
Lies beneath a shimmering haze
From sun flecked vapour spun it seems
Unreal a myth before my gaze

2

An iridescent fragment chipped
From off a drifting cloud on high
That in descent became gold tipped
Brushed by the sun as it passed by

3

The landmarks that I know so well
Have been transformed and now appear
So different I cannot tell
What magic has been working here

4

In Phoenix Park the monument
A cellar filled with glistening salt
These changes by the distance lent
I view with wonder as I halt

5

Upon the climbing mountain path
That leads to Hellfire and Glencree
And from a nearby faery rath
I hear the voices of the shee

6

Gasometers one grey two red
The swirling wreaths of mist enfold
Shining spools of silken thread
Their silvered rims shot through with gold

7

The housing schemes that now replace
The fields of green and country lanes
Their coloured roofs now interlace
To form a patchwork and the panes

8

Of many windows turned to gold
Steeped in a yellow sunlight flood
A jewelled myriad doth hold
Shining sapphires, rubies of blood

9

Over the roofs of houses stand
Church spires reaching to the sky
Sentinels watching o' er the land
The symbols of our Deity

10

Smoke belching forth from chimneys tall
In curling clouds of grey ascends
It forms a gilt edged purple pall
As with the golden haze it blends

11

A giant fish with lacquered fin
Lies upon a somnolent sea
The Hill of Howth where once proud Finn
Hunted and hosted with the shee

12

The daylight now begins to fade
Azure and gold deepen above
A soft subduing sombre shade
Sweeps o' er the city that I love

Published: Ireland' s Own, January 12, 1952

Ceilidhe

1
I could not be present there that night
But you were there
Sweet strains of music lilting and light
Over the air
Were borne to me; I sat desolate

2
The radio impersonal cold
Failed to create
The warm magic atmosphere of old
It was too late
But no, the music it was changing

3
It was my favourite dance they played
A reel for two
And I, no longer alone, I stayed
But came to you
You clasped my hand, we were together

4
Tirelessly we danced until the dawn
Our spirits high
Silver slights were streaking o' er the lawn
Of crystal sky
You kissed me then and thus we parted

5
The music now had ceased a voice cut through
My futile dream
Announcing a group of songs and two
With love the theme
I switched it off, a click, then silence

6
Yes tirelessly you would dance till dawn
But not with me
Held safe within your arms at break of morn
I would not be
But lying awake vainly weeping

Contrasts

1

A turquoise moon in a sky of flame
A winter' s day that seemed almost spring
A mild breeze pregnant with coming rain
A bird from a naked perch did sing

2

The mountains brooding sombrely lay
Etched in the orange glare of the sky
Above which the clouds hung heavy and grey
Piled in threatening banks on high

3

The trees by pilfering gales stripped bare
Drenched in an eerie brilliance stood
Their leafless branches the tangled hair
Of spectres caught in a red gold snood

4

A veil from silver amethyst spun
Concealing the twilight' s purple gown
In filmy folds around her hung
Pale herald of the night to come

5

The lingering day seemed loathe to leave
As slowly she wound her silken skeins
Translucent strands twinning twilight's sleeve
The fraying fragments of broken dreams

6

Refreshed from resting on yonder hill
From slender moorings drifted the clouds
Hastening their crystal contents to spill
The silver tassels from day' s pale shard

7

From out the Heavens all colour fled
The mountains, the trees and sky all grey
Rain—washed, desolate, their beauty shed
In mourning the passing of the day

Brevity

How precious were the moments shared
With you each day
The little things for which you cared
I stored away

To keep for you
The poem in the book I read
At home last night
The beauty on your hilltop shed

By pale moonlight
I shared with you
I climbed Howth's summit and I thought
I'll tell to him

How heather scented breezes brought
The deeds of Finn
So close to me
How rushing past me Grainne fair

Had turned to speak
With Diarmuid and her flying hair
Caressed my cheek
She smiled at me

Discussing plays we both had seen
Exchanging views
On places where we both had been
Glencree, Glendubh

Brought joys untold
From sunrise over Kevin's bed
We promised soon
To watch until the peaks turned red

Under the moon
Of burnished gold
Beneath the leafless trees we walked
And watched the spring

Creep on their branches and we talked
Of many things in Stephen's Green
And then I'd think within my heart
This soon must end

A little while and we will part
And I'll pretend
It was but a dream

Togher

1

Two black birds in a sky of blue
Silently winged their homeward way
Over the hills of smokey hue
Steeped in lingering shades of day

2

A lane that wound its mossy way
Through hedges rich in gorse of gold
Through fields where daffodils held sway
Where lambs played truant rom their fold

3

By brown gurgling mountain streams
Past houses where we mortals dwell
Dreaming those ever futile dreams
Then on towards a faery dell

4

Where wee folk dance beneath the moon
Around an ancient tree of thorns
Upon a verdant carpet strewn
With silver cones and gold acorns

5

Then past an old grey church of stone
Slumbering on a grassy knoll
There smoking his pipe all alone
The sexton leaned against the wall

6

And finally it petered out
Vanishing where the main road ran
A fragile dream a whispered shout
Lost in a chaos made by man

Lough Tay

1

Small silver speckled stones were strewn
Upon a shining stretch of sand
A silent stretch wherein the tune
Of birds seemed hushed by some command

2

The crystal waters of Lough Tay
Washed gently o' er this sequinned beach
Around which fine clad slopes gave way
To bare blue hills that sought to reach

3

The azure realms of the sun
Peeping in patches through the cloud
That swirling round their summits spun
For each proud peak a gold flecked shroud

4

I sat and gazed upon this scene
And gazing, time for me stood still
Till life seemed but a passing dream
And Heaven just beyond yon hill

Musings in Malady

1

I like it not this being in bed
A lengthy spell
I must have rest the doctor said
Before I' m well
I like it not

2

A vase of flowers beside the bed
My only link
With symphonies of summer sped
Too soon I think
For me to grasp

3

Blossoms shot with incandescent hues
From sun distilled
Pastel shades of yellows merge with blues
My room is filled
With fragrance sweet

4

This myriad of maytime flowers
Transport me far
Away from city streets and dreary hours
That tend to mar
My soul' s content

5

Fields and lush green meadows saw their birth
On distant hills
Where birdsong throbs with riotous mirth
And mature thrills
To its gay lilt

6

Summer shall have gone ere I arise
To venture forth
Phoebus shall have flown from out the skies
And from the north
Cold winds will blow

Words

1
Words fascinate me and assume
Within my mind
Size colour shape and tone to tune
With what I find
I have to say

2
Like pieces of a jigsaw game
They came apart
Then form a pattern when again
I make a start
Each to replace

3
I sort and string them in a line
Until I make
One sentence with another rhyme
And then I break
And make again

4
With laughter I can make them lilt
Or let them fall
Like tender tears of sorrow spilt
On youth's pale pall
Of broken dreams

5

A word that can with anguish sound
So desolate
Could change with love's fulfilment found
And life vibrate
With happiness

6

Like destiny with words I play
She plays with men
I use each one and then I lay
It back again
She does the same

Repatriation

1

There is a land to which I often travel
When fate has been unkind
The tangled threads of life fail to unravel
And peace of mind
Becomes a farce

2

It is a land of muted muddied colour
A dreary dismal place
And those who tread its shores of grief and squalor
A shipwrecked race
Doomed to despair

3

It is a land where youthful hopes are shattered
Where striving seems futile
Perfection looms, a goal round which is scattered
A pathetic pile of lost ideals

4

And to this land of darkness where I'm gated
No ray of light may prod
There I must stay until repatriated
By thou my God
And welcomed home

Tyrolean Rose

1

Deep in a box of old forgotten treasures
A rose doth lie
Conjuring up bright visions of past pleasures
When youth and I
Walked hand in hand

2

This blossom bloomed within an
Alpine garden
In far Tiról
Until a boy, of nature asking pardon
Approached and stole
From her this rose

3

This was a night when
Tyroleans went dancing
Dressed in their best
Feathered caps and dark eyes boldly glancing
For some conquest
To grace the ball

4

Marching through the village merrily singing
Torches aflame
The echo of their laughter gaily ringing
From chain to chain
Of snow capped peaks

5

And with this band where youth predominated
Marched the boy
The rose he plucked in his cap now decorated
And passing by
The cheering crowds

6

He saw a wistful stranger and he offered
To her his arm
He took and kissed the rose then shyly proferred
With old world charm
This primal pledge

7

I sadly close the box where it is lying
Faded and crushed
And out across the years my heart is crying
Caught in a rush
Of memories

Published: Cork Weekly Examiner July 26, 1952

Church music in Tiról

The strains of a violin
Slender silvery
Merged with the notes
The deep notes

Of cello and organ
A combination
Of exquisite harmony
Filling the church

O' er flowing and spilling
Into the open
A galaxy of sounds
Sweet and poignant

And from the mountains
An echo exultant
Was flung
Bridging the chasms

With woof hymeneal
And the birds
In thrilling cadences
Paid tribute

To this man—made music

Paris—a trio

From the air I first beheld her
Steeped in the August sunshine
A closely woven tapestry
Of grey and green and red

Her pattern broken
By the long silver thread
Of the river Seine
And the gilded black

Of the Eiffel Tower
This was Paris
The excitement at the airport
The bus ride to the terminal

The tantalising glimpses
Of things so strange and new
And the mad melee of the traffic
The fascinating cafés

Beneath their striped awnings
An appetising aroma
Of coffee black and strong
And the long thin rolls

Of fresh white bread
The gesticulating gendarmes
Thin dark eyes boldly glancing
The handsome youth who smiled at me

In the place de la Concorde
And the sweet fragrance
Of hidden violets
The walk by the river Seine

Slumbering in the sunlight
Along her banks fond lovers
Kissed and made their vows
In front of Notre Dame

An artist sketched
The immenseness of the station
They call the Gare de l' Est
The overcrowded buffet

A second Tower of Babel
And the French soldiers
Gay, bantering
Thus was Paris

From the air I last beheld her
In the fitful sunshine gleams
Of a wet autumnal day
Gay, irresistible

Vowing to return
Blinded by a rush of tears
I softly whispered
An au revoir
That was Paris

46

The Vale of Laragh

A blue silver radiance
Distilled from the sky
From the inky velvet sky
Sequin star studded

Drenched the earth with brilliance
And the mountains lay
Like giant sapphires
Beneath its glow

An orchestration of sound
Tumultuous ecstatic
Poured from the fine wood
Claiming an echo

From the valleys and mountains
And filling the night
With passionate nocturne
Of mating birds

Laden with myriad scents
A warm heady wind
Caressed the tall trees
Crooned through the bushes

Through the golden gorse bushes
Crouched by the roadside
And swept silently
Through the long grass

The cry of a curlew
Rose from the marshes
A sad eerie cry
Wistful, desolate

And the great pulse of the hills
Throbbed in sympathy
And I, thinking of you
I too was sad

Lough Dan

1

Swirling scarves of grey gossamer
Draping the purple of the hills
Touching the waters of the lake
With trailing fringes
And ruffling its placid surface
Now suffused in misty pearl
Through a rift in the clouded sky
A single ray of light appeared
Etching in its pale gleam a boat
Headed shoreward
Flicking the lacy mist with gold
Then diminishing in darkness
Soon the hills were shrouded in gloom
The lake beneath a leaden sky
Was hidden by driving rain
And all was silent
Save for the dripping sound on the leaves
And the mournful bleating of sheep

2

The lake a pool of silvered gold
Bathed in brilliant sunshine lay
Mirroring in its shivering depths
A host of colours
The rich warm tints of the hills
And the pastels of the sky
A silver streamlet from the lake
Meandered on through furzeland
And in the wooded slopes above
Mountainy sheep
Were grazing and the young lambs
Tumbled through the tall grass
This was Nature' s jour de fete
A gay carnival of colour
The sound of laughter was in the wind
Faery laughter
From far away, and from the woods
Spring' s sylvan symphony of song

A Thought

I do not think you ever loved me
And yet
You have given me so much
And I
I have always loved you
I have given you everything
But you
You have received nothing
Because
You never knew

Thoughts and Tears

Shall I ever walk in the hills again
And feel soft breezes blowing through my hair
And know the gentle kisses of the rain
The perfume laden kisses of the air

Shall I see Tibradden's slopes no more
As last I saw them dressed in robes of spring
Or watch the lark into heavens soar

And think of what fair realms does he sing
Or shall I walk beneath a summer sky
And see the hills with splendour all ablaze
And o'er the city sweeping from on high

The golden glory of a summer haze
Or watch the larches swaying in the wind
And listen to the whispering of leaves
The sombre leaves that shape the mountain pines

Or rest in lonely glens where moon—light sleeps
Or standing in the forest watch the trees
Turn to gold beneath and autumn sun
Filtering through the russet of the leaves

Gilding gossamer webs by spiders spun
Or shall I stand within a field of snow
And see the Hellfire dark against the sky
A winter' s sky suffused with crimson glow

With banks of snow cloud piling up on high
I see them now beneath a haze of blue
Changing through the seasons through the years
And thinking of the hills I think of you
And find myself remembering with tears

Published: Cork Weekly Examiner, October 11, 1952; Rosc, March, 1953

To Shakespeare

Into the mouth of every player
You have put
Such words of wisdom
And yet
Every play
Is but a tragedy
Yes
Even your comedies
Are tragic
For in portraying the lighter side of life
You have revealed
The darkness beyond

Reception

The tapestry of life
Is woven in the sky
The ever changing tapestry
Of light and shade
A kaleidoscope of contrasts

Portraying man' s many moods
From Trenanen
The roseate tints of the sky
Reflect in the waters of the sea
Painting its so still surface

In shades of silvered rose
And the dark silhouettes
Of houses and trees
Sun etched in ebony
A cock crows

The scene changes
No longer cold, calm and remote
But warm and stirring
Above the colours deepen
A grey cloud folds back

Revealing a patch of azure
And the sun
Spilling his yellow liquid
Transforms the land and the sea
Till all become enchanted
Beneath a mist of gold

Greystones

Beneath the summer sky
The sea was golden blue
The boat was drifting
And you and I

Were talking
The waves murmured gently
Making a lapping noise
Overhead the gulls

Were circling
And crying
Then you were singing
And over the water

The sound of your voice
Through the silence
Was carried
You laughed and from the hills

The echo of laughter
Was borne on the breeze
The breeze that tossed
Your brown hair

You rowed and the boat sped
Swiftly over the waves
The blue dancing waves
And the oars beat

Steadily
On through a swirling haze
Of golden enchantment
Faster and faster

We went skimming
Endlessly

Wings

The cry of the gulls at dawn
Shrill piercing
Filled with longing
The distant places

For the sea
The siren sea
That tosses them
Shamelessly

From wave to wave
On the rocks
Where they perch
Proudly

Over the city they fly
Circling restlessly
And their cry is filled
With a strange unquiet

Then they are gone
Leaving me
Shaken
Filled with restless yearning

For far distant places
For winged freedom
And you
The sky is filled with gold

A pale pink
Flushes
The grey cheeks of dawn
And the gulls

They have wings
And are unfettered

Blue, green and grey

A faint blue outline
Rising above
The grey crooked roofs
Of the houses

Framed by the leaves
Of two tall trees
And the sombre dwellings
Of the city

Were no more
The noise of the traffic
Was muted
The passers by
Gone

I was alone
No, not quite alone
The wild vagrant spirit
Of the mountains
Embraced me
And I responded
Passionately

The impudent breeze
That dwells
In high places
Tossed my hair

Then kissed me
Mockingly
And his kiss
Was cool, firm and tender
And his breath
Was laden
With myriad scents

I trembled
And the vagabond song
Of the hills
Beat
In my heart
Beside me
A bus shrieked to a standstill

And the precious moment
Torn
From the grasping hands
Of time
Was being
Reclaimed

Loss is gain

Sometimes
To lose
Is to have forever

Sometimes
To possess
Is to destroy
Forever

The life
Of a flower
When plucked
Is short

And love
Like a flower
Is fragile

19 Ely Place

I thought
Everything
Is just
The same

And yet
Something
Was different
Something
Had changed

Yes
It was I
I who was different
I who had changed
So much

And yet
So little

This poem referred to the Dublin address of the Five Provinces' branch of the Gaelic League, of which Bernadette was a dedicated member in her younger days

Three tenses

I walked
Into
The present
Making plans
For the future

When everything
That is
Or could be
Was
In the past

A Transient Flame

The alchemist of autumn
Was in the green today
I saw him swinging from a branch
I heard him pipe a lay

And as he swung from branch to branch
The leaves were shaken down
To form a chequered tapestry
Of yellow green and brown

He danced upon the fallen leaves
And vainly sought to hold
His ever trailing mantle
Of flame and russet gold

Upon the cool capricious breeze
The words he sang were borne
A wild weird whisper through the trees
As though he wished to mourn

The ephemeral beauty
Of things that pass away
The idyllic dance of the may fly
Danced on a summer day

And woven through his pipings
The sadness of a world
Where fallen leaves of autumn
Follow buds of spring unfurled

Published: Cork Weekly Examiner November 1, 1952

A Holocaust of Leaves

Heaped beside the grass
In charred and blackened piles
The burned leaves lay
Leaves that were part

Of spring' s green freshness
Of summer' s sensuous splendour
Of autumn' s golden glory
Now lay

Smouldering
The funeral pyres
Of a dying year
And with them lay

The eager aspirations
Of a springtime
A summer' s brief fulfilment
An autumn' s sad maturity

Ashes all

Published:Rosc, January, 1953

Oidhche

Oidhche Chorringhthe
Id theannta
Ag déanamh baoth—chainnte
Gan brígh

Ag déanamh grádh
Gan toradh
Oidhche mhi—shuaimhneach
Gan codhladh

Ag iarraidh éalódh
Óm smaointe
Ag iarraidh éalódh
Ón saoghal

Maidin trom liath
Gan faoisimh
Ag féachaint ar aghaidh
Go sochtach
Ag feiscint

Tada

Published: Rosc, January, 1953; Irishwoman's Journal, March 1966

67

Silvered Darkness

Caught in the folds of a cloud
The pale November moon
Gleamed eeriely
A soft rain was falling

And the pools on the pavement
Were filled with moonlight
With white silver moonlight
A breeze swept down from the hills

The clouds were blown
And the captive moon released
Dappled with silver
The bare black branches

Of the trees
Festooned with quivering raindrops
The crystallised tears of the gods
Shed at the birth of winter

From skies of winter

A scintillating haze
A sky of saxe and pearl
Shot through with flicks of gold dust
From the rising sun

A ball of molten gold in the east
A fleet of foamy clouds
Upon a sea blue sky
Fringed with radiant edges

Etched faintly in the gleam
Of the pale and wintry sunshine
A tracery of black
Against a sky of bronze

With turquoise tinted patches
Peeping through the clouds
Peeping through the buff and burnished clouds
A silver filigree

A grey amthyst sky
With clouds of black and purple
Moored on sea green strings
To the far west of the horizon

The Mist

The black naked skeletons
Of winter's wind whipped trees
Were swathed in swirling vapour
Curling around

Their shorned branches
Embracing
Their rain washed bodies
It swept sinuously

Along the ground
Trailing wispy fingers
Through wind wearied grasses
Draping haze black bushes

In blue grey gossamer
Then drifting wraith like
Through the trees
Now shadowy and unsubstantial
In the eerie half light

The Moon

The moon a disc of glimmering gold
Was tossed into the blue air
And there
Floated lightly

Passing beneath
A puff of pearl grey vapour
Drifting into
The bare beckoning branches

Of a tall tree
Held for a moment
In a clan—like embrace
And then
Sent spinning into space

Draíocht

Gaethe órdha na gréine
Ag sleamhnú that dhruim an t—slé
Dorchadas na h—oiehe
Ag tuitim go mall réidh.

Ciúneas draíochta an ghleanna,
Ag brú isteach orainn araon,
Sionsarnail na gaoithe
Tré ghéaga loma crainn.

Aoibhneas agus iontas
Teangmháil ár mbéal,
Solas séimh na réalt
Am' tharraing I bhfad ón saol.

Smaointe aite raigneacha,
Ón aimsir atá thart,
Ag bagairt are mo shuaimhneas,
Ag glacadh uaim mo neart.

Published:Rosc, March, 1953; Irishwoman's Journal, August, 1966

72

Caprice

In Dresden dirndl sprigged with white
She came through winter still remained
Her breath was cool her kiss was light
And in her glance a promised reigned

She wandered softly through the trees
Touching their branches bruised and bare
A coronet of pale green leaves
Was clasped around her golden hair

She wooed the earth from slumber deep
With snatches of enchanted song
Frail snowdrops from the ground did peep
To watch her as she danced along

Gathering sunbeams as she went
With aery tread from tree to tree
While they their bare black branches bent
To form a fragile filigree

A fragrant rain fell from above
Splashing with silver her golden hair
The kisses of the gods who love
In main this siren maid so fair

Then twirling lightly on her toes
She wandered back from whence she came
Winter with his retinue rose
To claim his kingdom once again

But he no longer reigned supreme
For earth had wakened from his trance
Had seen a vision in his dream
Had seen a promise in her glance

Published:Rosc, April, 1953; Cork Weekly Examiner, February 28, 1953

A Decade

Down through the tunnel of the years
A single ray of light appears
Then eagerly I seek to find
That something which is hid behind
The thick impenetrable veil
Hiding its source but yet I fail
Crying aloud in my despair
I find the light no longer there
Only the darkness and the fears
Down through the tunnel of the years

Published: Rosc, May, 1953

Waste

I squander the present
Peering ahead
Over the crescent
Of the years
Turning the future
Founded on fears
Into the past
Consumed with dread
I squander the present

Adrift

Flung from a vessel of dreams
Into realitys sea
I flounder in the deep depression
Of its waters
And see

The wreckage of each ideal
Sweeping past
I vainly seek to grasp
Each drifting moment

But caught in lifes current
Am swept out of reach
I try to find a foothold
On the beach of Immortality

But perish
In a whirlpool
Of emotion

In the Half Light

The trees stood out
In the still air
Like patterned silhouettes
Against a heavy hazed sky

And there
Away from humanity's shout
We walked
You and I

Over the dew drenched grass
Your hand in mine
We seemed to pass
Out of place
Out of time

Spring is Fey

With quickened pulse and arms outstretched
Expectancy in every glance
The adolescent spring has fetched
Pale leaves and flowers to advance

The golden glory of her hair
The sylvan splendour of her gown
Fragrant fragile fey and fair
Awaits fulfilment that will come

When clasped in summer' s warm embrace
In the white heat of noonday sun
Drugged with joy she sees no trace
Of autumn' s ills or winter' s tomb

No Twilight

This night a game of make—belief has ended
I will make believe I' m glad
When all the things that you and
I pretended
Shall come to make me sad

When autumn hides beneath her tattered splendour
The disillusioned spring
I shall recalled the joys of last
September
To swiftly vanishing

The joys that through the winter months have lasted
The moments dark and bright
When summer ran to meet the spring we parted
The day has turned to night

Bleakness

The bare bleak buttress of the future
Juts out across the the summit of the years
A cold grey wall of stone looms ahead
And I am filled with dread and countless fears
For I can see no path where I might tread
No foothold that might ease this arduous climb
Only the bare bleak buttress of the future
Interminably stretching into time

A Fragment

Spring gathered blossoms in her skirt
Her skirt of palest greens
Then laughing loud with childish mirth
She filled my life with dreams
Spring shook the blossoms from her skirt
Her skirt of palest greens
Then laughing with unholy mirth
She snatched from me my dreams

A Sonnet

A slender sliver of moon curved gold
Hung on a silver chain from the neck of night
And from her ears a set of sapphire stars
A bouquet of pale blossoms she did hold
A fragrant fragile froth of pink and white

A faint breeze through her raven tresses stirred
Tossing the crown of cloudlets on her head
Swirling the blue green mantle round her feet
Painting in purple patches the long grass
And from the drifting blossoms newly shed

Arose an eary perfume heady sweet
A vision of silvered whiteness night had passed
Leaving me desolate weary racked with pain
Seeking to forget, I sought in vain.

The Tear

I watched a raindrop poised upon a leaf
Translucent crystal clear
Of exquisite beauty its reign was brief
This celestial tear
To earth by a thoughtless breeze was blown
To splash in silvered fragments o' er the grass
Moments such as this I too have known
Exquisite fragile moments that swiftly pass

The Alien

I have shared dreams with spring
Frail lovely impossible dreams of youth
The dreams to which we cling
While seeking, finding losing beauty truth

With autumn I have mourned
The heartbreak of a disillusioned spring
And with her I have borne
The fears of what the years ahead may bring

With winter I have lain
With her I waited in the cold grey tomb
There filled with fear and pain
I waited for the spectre death to come

Summer remains unknown
Sensuous season of satiety
Your fate I cannot morun
Fulfilment you have never shared with me

Published:Rosc, August/ September, 1953

Light and Shade

The breeze was chasing shadows through the grass
White clouds were trailing streamers in the blue
They tossed them to the sun and as they passed
A golden glance to each of them he threw

A stream was holding captive in its bed
The trembling pale reflection of the sky
With swift and swaying motion overhead
The mayflies came to dance to love, to die

The mountains dark with anger when the breeze
Ruffled the smoothness of their summer greens
Were soothed by the sun that through the trees
Kissed their darkened brows with golden gleams

The breeze in impish mood had from the flowers
Stolen sweet scents and carried everywhere
A pilfered load of sweetness that in showers
Of haunting fragrance filled the summer air

A feast of birdsong floating from the trees
An echo from the distant hills did raise
That merging with the murmering of leaves
Became a symphony of joy and praise

A sad spectator at this joyous fete
I watched the summer pageantry sweep past
I watched and mourned the tragedy of fate
That mars all beauty with an icy blast

Published: Rosc, August/ September, 1953; Cork Weekly Examiner, June 27, 1953

The Pier

The sun was slowly sinking from our sight
Grey gulls were drifting on a calm green sea
The day was quietly yielding to the night
Embraced by him she almost ceased to be

The sun trailed golden fingers through the waves
Stirring their grey green depths with myriad gleams
The hills were shrouded in a light blue haze
The city lay beneath a pall of dreams

Far out to sea white yachts stood motionless
Etched in the bronzed light of the setting sun
The fishermen were hauling in their nets
Smiling content their day' s work almost done

Soon sea and sky were washed with greyish light
To the far west of the horizon' s rim
The sun still flaunted in the face of night
A gaudy and gold scarf to anger him

The darkness swept across the faded sky
And through the blue black curtain of the night
Pale stars began to peer and passing by
Small boats were sprinkled with fragmented light

Together we were part of this strange scene
Of sea and sky in the jewelled arms of night
Yet now it seems as though twere but a dream
An idyllic dream dispensed by dawn' s cold light.

Published: Cork Weekly Examiner, August 8, 1953

Summer Breeze

O wild mischievous summer breeze
From what far off mysterious clime
Have you imparted to the trees
Strange tales that make them all the time

With ceaseless chatterings commune
As if by some excitement swayed
They dance to an enchanted tune
By your strange unseen retinue played

They dance and wave their leafy limbs
With wild and weird abandoned glee
Incited by the heady hymns
The incantations of the shee

Impetuous wooer of the flowers
What fascinating force is yours
What contents in your crystal showers
Create the visions that will lure

Fragile blossoms to open wide
Their tender hearts to your caress
To tremble neath the raging tide
Of fierce wild passion when you press

Upon each petal warm and bright
A demonic destroying kiss
Leaving them drugged with delight
Spent with extremity of bliss

Then off you flit to distant groves
While wilting on the grass they lie
One never loves until one loves
And yet to love is but to die

Published: Cork Weekly Examiner, September 5, 1953

The Wood

A hidden pool with magic in its depth
A mirror for the tall and trembling trees
Through which pale shafts of sun and shadows crept
To peer at this reflection through the leaves

A wood that spread its dark mysterious growth
Beneath the gold and purple of the hills
When strange sounds oozed from every feathered throat
To fill the air with wild rapturous trills

The swarming flies were humming in their flight
While crawling insects buzzed upon the ground
The summer' s sylvan symphony of sight
Merged with a surging symphony of sound

Tall sun steeped trees were seeking to prolong
In vain fulfilments brief ecstatic spell
Their leafy branches to each other clung
Defying the chill of sudden rain that fell

Like lovers locked in desperate embrace
Sensing the autumn of their love draw near
Thinking to stay awhile life's waning pace
They live with the intensity of fear

All nature seemed pulsating with this life
Vibrating with the need of her desires
The hectic urge to live when time is brief
Soon winter's urn would hold spent summer fires.

Published: Cork Weekly Examiner, September 19, 1953

Shadows

The mountains rising out of the mist
Like half formed dreams
Were floating in air, azure air, kissed
By golden gleams

Over the sea where white wavelets danced
Where grey gulls cried
Over the sea where pale sunbeams glanced
On an ebbing tide

Out of a swirling grey blue haze
Their shapes were born
Then lost as into the swirling haze
They did return

The mountains fading into the mist
Like half formed dreams
Were floating in air no longer kissed
By golden gleams

The End

Grey silver moonlight
Crept across the sand
Out of the dark night
Away from the land
Down to where white waves

Kissed the sleeping shore
Soft silvery waves
Sad slumbering shore
Moved by the magic
Of moonlight on sand

Thrilled by the tragic
The touch of your hand
A brave brief pretence
Poor frail ghost of love.

Leaves

The debris of the autumn on the grass
Blown upon a hectic breeze soon spent and still
The tawny tattered splendours of her dress
No longer lay like gold on every hill

But torn to shreds upon the ground it lay
Sodden and muddied by the heavy rain
A black and yellow pulp of damp decay
Mourned by the lonely leaves that did remain

Clinging in desperation to each branch
Bruised by the breeze drenched by the driving rain
O loyal leaves so stoic and so staunch
Twere better far to go than to remain

Pitiful plaything of the cruel wind
Your comrades ceased to struggle and are free
But foolishly you sought to stay behind
Softly sighing to soothe each aching tree

But soon strong winds will
Sweep you to the ground
In fierce and fitful gusts that tired of play
Will sweep your battered forms onto the mound

Where other leaves lie rotting in decay
But phoenix like your forms will know rebirth
The sun will shine the birds will start to sing
When hesitant you reappear on earth

The poignant pleasures of another spring.
One Sunday Night
Dark chimney tops against a lurid sky
Watched by a troubled moon with clouded brow

Washed by the rain that fell while you and I
Stood beneath a tree whose trembling bough
Caught in the frenzied clutches of the breeze
Shaken by the squalls of heavy hail

Shook and scattered from its tortured leaves
Showers of chilling raindrops while the gale
Swirling around is tossed into the air
Our whispered words pregnant with fear and pain

Tossing and hurling back from everywhere
Infused with echoes every drop of rain
All nature seemed to tremble with unrest
Tempestuous and wild she sought to cling

To passing summer writhing in protest
Yet she will always know another spring

One Sunday Night

Dark chimney tops against a lurid sky
Watched by a troubled moon with clouded brow
Washed by the rain that fell while you and I
Stood beneath a tree whose trembling bow

Caught in the frenzied clutches of the breeze
Shaken by the squalls of heavy hail
Shook and scattered from its tortured leaves
Showers of chilling raindrops while the gale

Swirling around us tossed into the air
Our whispered words pregnant with fear and pain
Tossing and hurling back from everywhere
Infused with echoes every drop of rain

All nature seemed to tremble with unrest
Tempestuous and wild she sought to cling
To passing summer writhing in protest
Yet she will always know another spring

Still Life

A canvas stretched across the endless years
Lifeless and dull and grey
An empty palette washed by futile tears
Devoid of colour lay

Beside the broken brushes of the past
Each strand a lost ideal
That failed to paint a picture that would last
One perfect and yet real

You brought me colours that were gay and bright
You taught me how to form
A living pattern from each day and night
A shelter from life' s storm

I piled my canvas high and did not spare
The precious paints you gave
I lived, I loved I lost I now despair
No colour did I save

I tried to change the pattern when you went
To wash away with tears
The coloured days and nights together spent
To wash away the fears

I left my canvas colourless and base
My palette empty too
Impossible to paint a picture there
With colours that are new

Published: Cork Weekly Examiner, April 10, 1954

The Aftermath

How bitter are the berries of regret
How heavily they hang upon life's tree
How sweet the seeds of folly are, and yet
Its fruits are fear, frustration, misery
A shower of silvery moments
Splashed from the clouds of time
Brief misted mercurial moments
That now and then are mine

The Reprieve

That night
We kissed as though each kiss might be the last
That night
We clung as if in clinging close and fast

We might prolong the moment's exhultation
A moment snatched from hours of desolation
That night
Was charged with wild despair and desperation

The Pendulum

Two windows flank the doorway of my mind
There are two windows in the walls of time
From one the past peers through a broken blind
Some panes are bright some cracked and dull with grime
The second one is paned with misted glass

Through which the happenings of future years
As tantalising shadows flit and pass
The disembodied myths the hopes the fears
The doorway to the present lies between
At each essayed approach I deviate

There like a reed I back and forth and lean
The past repels the future fascinates
From out the present every joy is cast
I fear the future then regret the past.

Published: Cork Weekly Examiner, May 22, 1954

The Purge

Love found me wandering lost in the night
I followed him thinking to find the dawn
That lurked in the strange evanescent light
Surrounding the shape of his shadowed form

Love took me captive, he held me in chains
Leaving me locked in a cell of despair
He looked through the grill and laughed at my pains
Untouched by my tears unmoved by my prayer

Love gave me wings and he taught me to fly
Then mocked at my efforts to break down the bars
That stood between me and the beckoning sky
That stood between me and the way to the stars

Love was my goaler but now
I am free
To shake off the shackles of memory.

Published: Cork Weekly Examiner, July 3, 1954

Death?

The coffin of the past is filled with dreams
Dreams that shroud the mouldering corpse of love
Whose spirit through the clay of time still gleams
Hovering near the withered wreaths above
A fragile ghost that haunts in retrospect

Reprocheful of my efforts to forget
Its presence lingers seeming to erect
A tombstone time has fashioned from regret
Idyllic and ephemeral the phase
When love had promised life and happiness

If weeping could this memory erase
Perhaps the pain of parting would grow less
One' s epitaph is written through the years
Indelible the ink in vain the tears.

Expiation

Within the courtroom of the mind
I stand
By all the jury of my thoughts condemned
The actions of the past are near at hand

They mock my every effort to defend
Each one bears witness to the awful wrong
Love was the victim folly was the crime
I did but end in seeking to prolong

In frantic fear I watched its swift decline
A fragile flower I watched it fade and die
While held too tightly in my eager grasp
I watched the petals of its life drift by

To settle on the debris of the past
When sentenced to a life of vain regret
How futile seem my efforts to forget.

The Rainpool

I almost walked on the sky today
A pool of blue on a path of grey
Some gold green leaves were fluttering round
This patch of azure upon the ground

The foam of cloudlets while drifting past
Flecked lady images through the grass
And cut from their foamy filigree
A hesitant sunbeam stooped to see

A gilded reflection framed in cloud
That faintly within the rainpool glowed
Beneath an eager shower of rain
Shot through with silver the gold became

A shimmering pool of liquid light
A sensuous scintillated sight
Brushed by the lips of a passing breeze
Shivered and splintered with ecstasy

Scattering silvery fragments round
The gilded globules upon the ground
Released by the parting clouds the sun
No longer hesitant boldly shone

Soon under its brash apppraising gaze
The pool became a winnowing haze
Retreating from the fluttering leaves
Vanished in vapour upon the breeze

Published: Cork Weekly Examiner, September 18, 1954

Intrusion

Spinx—like my tortured heart keeps asking why
Insatiate absorbing each reply
While I can only answer with my tears
The past returns to mock my weary years
The past returns to be my future guest

And I must entertain him without rest
Excessive his demands and I must yield
Reopening a wound time has not healed
Unwelcome is this guest yet he stays on
Refusing to depart though spring has gone

The spring when life and love were both my guests
They left together with my happiness
The past has now removed the sign "to let"
I must collect the rent of my regret

Published: Cork Weekly Examiner, October 16, 1954

108

Too Late

Love cool and clinical
Bitter and cynical
Love curt and critical
Love analytical

Barred by cold purity
Love in obscurity
Marred by maturity
Seeking security

Love real yet mythical
Youth is incritical
Ruined by reality
Breeding banality

Love's bloom has turned to seed
Love's flower grown to weed

Sacrifice

Sudden resemblance of summer's spring
Weary suddenly ceased to cling
To trees that cried out in their pain
Fulfilment has been all in vain

The sensuous season of their lust
Had passed and in the acid dust
Of mutilated myths and dreams
They writhed and their tortured screams

That filled the darkness without cease
Were echoed by the mocking breeze
Their naked branches clawed the air
Abandoned desperate despair

Fevered frustrated filled with shame
Cowered beneath the squalls of rain
That spurted from the sullen sky
Like accusations from on high

Like lovers whose ecstatic phase
Has passed and in the greyish haze
Of disillusioned weariness
Cry out on fear and loneliness

Communion

They had no need for further false pretence
The naked souls that now stood face to face
Stripped bare of all their former reticence
Quivering with their eagerness did trace
Did trace and when they found did analyse

The fragile mechanism of the mind
Yet in this probing did not realise
That in some recess they would leave behind
The rubble of remembrance and the pain
The debris of a union that is brief

The traces of some spiritual shame
The seeking for deliverance the grief
The ecstasy of spiritual fusion
A self created myth a mere illusion

Pilgrimage

I sipped
The frosted champagne of the air
My spirits soared high
I skipped
Far over the well of despair

Neath the clear blue sky
We talked
It was Christmas time of the year
Before we found love
We walked

The hills seemed invitingly near
The sun shone above
We shared
So eagerly friendship of youth
Our laughter was gay

Unsmeared
By the loss of beauty and truth
That' s with us today
Today
It is Christmas time of the year

The ghosts of our love
Will stray
Where hills seemed invitingly near
Where sun shone above
In rain

A mist of great covers the hills
A drizzle of rain
Cold rain
From the dark and sullen sky spills
And deep is the pain

Nativity

Conceived in the womb of time
Brought forth in pain and in fear
At the sound of midnight' s chime
The babe of the future year
The heir to a mortgaged world

Built on a morass of strife
A puny mite it is hurled
Far into the stream of life
Bankrupt the old year has died
Leaving its newly born heir

Helplessly adrift on the tide
Near to the weir of despair
Twelve months come to drown or save
This ill—starred abandoned lake

Enigma

A world composed of winter dark and night
A world where I can see no spark of light
A world with which I can now longer cope
A world so utterly devoid of hope
A life from which all trace of love has flown

The harvest of regret by folly sown
For every moment borrowed out of time
I must repay in memory's bitter kine
What might have been extinguishes what is
And that which may be somehow fails to please

Accompanied by loneliness and fear
And yet alone I face each future year
The pattern of life's jig—saw must remain
A mystery I tried to solve in vain.

Aridity

The dawning of the day is dark
Dark and heavy the chilling rain
The wakening from sleep is stark
Stark with reality of pain
For in my dreams you had been near

Near was the hardness of your mouth
To my aching lips that now appear
Drawn with intensity of youth
Embraced content yet not content
With moments that the darkest night

From time outworn to me had lent
At dawn to vanish from my sight
Colourless dawn pitches rain
Banishing dreams, wakening pain

Isolation

The empty shells of vanished dreams
On the desolate sands of time
The tide of life no longer seems
To reach this narrow steep incline
The waters swirl around below

The flotsam in this narrow place
Remains immune to ebb and flow
Dank debris lying there trace
Fertile periods of the past
Before the past was cut adrift

Life' s singing seas now seldom cast
The spume of spray across the rift
The silent sounds of mute despair
The hovering in troubled air.

Tenacity

The soft caress of spring
Potent with unshed tears
Frail memories that cling
Like cobwebs through the years

Like cobwebs that have clung
To rafters out of reach
These memories have hung
Where time cannot impeach

In hiding they have hung
Until their fragile woof
Touched by quivering sun
That pierces winter' s roof

As drawn into the light
Each mote made to appear
A gilded globule caught
Remote yet very near

The memories we hold
Are in some recess trust
Until spring' s wand of gold
Transforms the dreaming dust

Fugue

The tragedy of spring when one is old
Is old and yet unable to forget
Flowers of beauty that once did unfold
The broken stems the harvest the regret
Unable to forget love's timeless birth

A love whose life tempestuous and short
Transformed the very essence of the earth
Into a substance charged with ageless mirth
Stifled within the grasp of greedy youth
Consumed within the flames of passion's fire

Cold shrouded in the shreds of tattered truth
Encompassed by the coffin of desire
The heartbreak of life's harvest in the fall
Hectic Halcyon days beyond recall

Cosmetics

The smeared—on lip stick will not hide
The piteous trembling of the mouth
Or stem the ever rising tide
Of misery or slake the drought
The desperate need to love to trust

To find a foothold on firm ground
To resurrect the buried dust
Of ideals lost beneath life' s mound
The powder puff will not efface
The ravages that time has worn

Or banish lines that grief did trace
To hide is never to adorn
The masquerade now nears an end
The final curtain soon descends

The Void

The loneliness the longing and the fear
That spring from an eternity of pain
The emptiness that grows with every year
The hopelessness the heartbreak all in vain
The terrible tenacity of thought

That trembles on the threshold of the mind
A web upon whose every strand is caught
Dust memories escaping leave behind
The loneliness adopted to conceal
The longing that can never be appeased

The fear that seems so vague and is so real
The groping in the darkness for release
The holocaust of happiness the fire
The raking of the ashes of desire

The Narcotic

The dreams that I have gathered through the years
Are spread upon the ground beneath your feet
Their trampled dust I moisten with my tears
I gather up the fragments and retreat
I strip my tortured soul and feel no shame

To lay it bruised and naked where you trod
Impervious to the cause of all its pain
With studied carelessness you probe and prod
You diagnose the cause but to prescribe
Is hopeless since you hold the power to cure

The healing draught I never shall imbibe
I may not live live or die I must endure
I hide behind a self created fence
I sicken of the drugs of my pretence

The Coffee Shop

Small and airless filled with smoke
Crowded to capacity
Young and careless students joke
Speaking with voracity

Drinking coffee puffing cigs
Lips from high stools dangling
Loath to wander back to digs
Poor food and constant wrangling

Dirty duffles drain pipe slacks
Proverbial regulation
Of the would be arty pack
The higher education

Decor in this pokey place
Is purely continental
On parle français in every space
The food is incidental

Waitresses are very grand
Haughty and superior
A certain type they seem to brand
Customers inferior

That is of the female sex
The males another matter
Nice and coy his wants they check
They simper and they chatter

They shake their heads and pat their hair
Like well fed kittens purring
They simply lavish him with care
The cause of all this stirring

The owner does not mind a bit
Her smile is sweet as honey
She' s tolerant and full of bliss
She' s thinking of the money

The Island

I hold a halfpenny in my hand
A rusty coin now wet with tears
I see again the golden sand
I think of all the empty years

Your flesh by sun and wind was tanned
The tang of salt was on your lips
Two strangers in a carefree land
The crying gulls the passing ships

Across the beach I watched you run
To where the sun seduced spray
Upon the waiting spray shore was flung
And there like silvered gold dust lay

You soon returned to hold me fast
With sea weed tangled in your hair
The seagulls cried this love must last
Love now replaced by cold despair

I hold a halfpenny in my hand
A rusty coin now wet with tears
You found it in the golden sand
I' ve kept it through the greying years

The Octopus

The tentacles of time are round me cast
Thin tentacles so short and yet so long
They reach out from the depths that is the past
Then backwards downwards slowly
I am drawn

I search within the armoury of mind
The present and the future empty lie
No weapon in their recess can I find
To reach a way to freedom and the sky
The life that permeates this sunken state

Is strange and filled with grotesque sounds and shapes
That through the waves of memory relate
And through the gap that is the present gape
The tides recede but there is left left behind
Dark water marks to stain a troubled mind

Poems

When I your mistress did become
Our mental intercourse was sweet
Our minds were fused the seeds were sown
The fertile seeds that soon would greet
The world in various forms of verse

The children of my teeming brain
Our union was so strange and terse
Their birth prolonged the parting pain
It seems impossible to hate
The children that are born of love

Yet they are guardians of the gate
Whose bars conceal the world above
I suffered that I might create
These images these forms of fate

The Jungle

The undergrowth of memory is filled
With strange and shapeless beasts of prey
Whose constant clamouring will not be stilled
Devouring every night and day
The present path that to the future leads

Is blocked by tangled hopes and fears
That grow upon the outskirts whose seeds
Are blown and scattered through the years
The foliage of fear has quickly spread
The leaves of hope are pinioned fast

Their roots are withered by the weeds of dread
That grow in thickets of the past
To hack a way to freedom I must find
Some implement embedded in the mind

Fathoms

The well of memory is running dry
I' ve drawn upon its waters through the years
There' s bitterness in tasting as I cry
Its shadowed contents mingle with my tears
The future well that springs from rocks of time

No longer flows a drought has marred its source
The trickle of the present the incline
The dam of fear the rapids of remorse
The flotsam left upon the river bed
The refuse of rembrance now embalmed

The petals of the present quickly shed
The ashes of the past is briefly fanned
The fraying strands that binds the ravelled rope
They strain against the jagged edge of hope

Published: Cork Weekly Examiner, July 9, 1955

Summer Sale

A cloudless sky of gentian hue
I turn in anguish from its sight
From air illumed with golden blue
I turn with longing to the night
The darkness where one need not hide
Unsightly scars of tortured hope
Or on the crest of envy ride
With happiness or try to cope
With worlds where people must not guess
What lies behind the false façade
There one pretends at happiness
That life is gay and one is glad
The milldew rot of unshed tears
Has spoiled the fabric of the years

Published: Cork Weekly Examiner, August 6, 1955

Bondage

I have loved and have been loved
Yet those I loved did not love me
I have been loved yet did not love
The ones who loved and were not free
If I should love one who did love
Then both as slaves we would be free
Then I would love and would be loved
The one I loved would too love me

The Quenching

The shed of time with sacks of seasons filled
Grey sacks that empty and deflated lie
Upon the ground their coloured contents spilled
The rainbow fragments of the dreams that die
Within the gate of life there is no fire

It holds the cluttered ashes of the past
They hide the broken bellows of desire
That on the future's empty hearth are cast
The cinders of regret will never burn
They're dampened by the drench of too much tears

The fuel of hope that feeds the present urn
Has dwindled with the usage of the years
There is no warmth in the tiny flame
That flickers through the iron bars of pain

Published: Cork Weekly Examiner, August 13, 1955

Formation

Tempers frayed and tenements
Dark memories of youth
Misery and discontent
Sans beauty and sans truth
Loneliness escorting fear

Inseparable from pain
Through each long and empty year
How steadfast they remain
Floundering and insecure
The helpless search to trust

Someone who would reassure
When dreams had turned to dust
Years of youth now old and soiled
Fabric of the future spoiled

Published: Cork Weekly Examiner, August 27, 1955

The Lack

All beauty from my weary world has flown
Even the hills can now no longer heal
The soothing spirit of the heights has shown
Indifference unheeding my appeal
The ever changing loveliness of skies
Reflected in the mirror of the seas
No longer makes my leaden heart to rise
The hopeless drifting of my thoughts to cease
The sound of running waters and the trills
Of birds rejoicing in their summer joy
No longer in my listless mind instils
Faint happiness it tend but to annoy
The mocking glance of sunshine' s golden ray
Can now no longer turn my night to day

No Credit

The shop of life with tempting stock is filled
Its spacious windows hold a vast display
That from the laden stands of time has spilled
To fall and lie in sumptuous array
I choose my favourite items with great care
I make believe I'm counting out the pence
To buy each piece of loveliness sold there
I only make a purchase of pretence
My quickened breath leaves shadows on the glass
Against which my distorted face is pressed
I look with longing for I soon must pass
Contented with a glimpse of happiness
I find it hard to tear myself away
Since I may not return another day

Terminus

I passed beyond the depths to where beneath
There flourishes the nightmare land of dreams
Inhabited by shades uncrowned by wreath
A land of darkness lit by greyish gleams
A land that knows no future, present past

A timeless planet drifting into space
From which all trace of human life is cast
The dwelling of a lifeless listless race
A child I use to dream of such a land
And from my sleep would blindly try to break

In terror vainly reaching out my hand
Now I have reached this land while still awake
Awake asleep and then to reawake
And from this sleep of wakefulness to break

Perhaps

I think
Tomorrow perhaps I will see him again
I blink
Back the tears as I think of the years of pain
I try to stifle the hope that is springing to life
I cry

With terror that tears through my mind like a knife
Afraid
That if I should regain once more I would lose
Afraid
Of the deepening pain of years of recluse

My heart
Is beginning to wake from its winter sleep
Yet part
Of its fragmented form still lies buried deep

Illumed
By the fire that springs from a rekindled dream
Consumed
By desire that clings to what once might have been

The Aerial

I sit and watch the drama of the years
Upon the television of the mind
It offers no relief to stem the tears
That well up from the depths and yet I find
A portrait of potential happiness
Unfinished scenes begin to end too soon
And then the hopeless hoping to possess
The wailing of earth's offspring for the moon
The fairy tales that reach no happy end
Across this narrow screen of life they flash
In broken sequence gaps that tend
But to portray the dreams that time has dashed
In search of skeep I turn the knob of night
Yet darkness cannot veil these scenes from sight

Published: Cork Weekly Examiner, November 10, 1955

The Serial

In youth I wrote of the land of faery
The ageless land of make—believe
Of the lilt of laughter light and aery
Where none was ever known to grieve

And then I idealised the mountains
The changing skies the tireless streams
The secret glades and the fickle fountains
With each I shared my doomed dreams

Now I can only write of the sorrow
That swept all beauty from the years
While today is yesterday's tomorrow
I hoped might give less cause for tears
Love is death is death in disguise

The Pattern

Tired of waiting watching hoping
Weary weeping tired of coping
Sick with longing lonely longing
Thoughts that tremble ever thronging

Warped with wishing woeful wishing
Downwards winged hopes go swishing
Sunshine through the darkness gleaming
Only comes in times of dreaming

Memories that mar the season
Pain predominates each season
Searing sorrow never ending
Each tomorrow still pretending

Petition

Love who metes out life and death
Fan me gently with your breath
If of life you will not give
Grant me death that I may live

Heartless you instil desire
Fanning flames you feed the fire
Heedless while you let it burn
Laughing as you fill life' s urn

Ruthless while with glee you gaze
On the flicker once a blaze
Stirring embers burning low
To the semblance of a glow

Love who metes out life and death
Fan me gently with your breath
If of life you will not give
Grant me death that I may live.

Published: Cork Weekly Examiner, November 19, 1955

Questionnaire

Our love be such
That one must suffer if one loves too much
Can love be vain
If one can love so much that love is pain
Can love be death
To make one die with every living breath
Can love be gay
That takes the brightness out of every day
Can love be right
To banish sleep from every lonely night
Can love be born
Of joy yet take the gladness from each morn
Can love be killed
Then every tender heartbeat must be stilled

Published: Cork Weekly Examiner, September 17, 1955

Illusion

Layers of gaiety I spread
To hide the hardness of the core
Of misery where love lies dead
Whose broken wings were made to soar
With laughter I must fill each day
The empty days that fill the years
Fake laughter lilting light and gay
Tremulous threaded through with tears
The wick of life is burning bright
Its lurid light will never last
To drive the darkness from the night
The empty lamp the shadows cast
No oil to feed the failing light
A flame a flicker fades from sight

Published: Cork Weekly Examiner, December 3, 1955

Striptease

Lost years of youth in wishing wasted
Life' s fruit was ever out of reach
The succulence that she once tasted
The tree is high and time can teach
The middle years the mad revision
Revising knowledge gleaned too late
Indifference and indecision
The final giving in to fate
The shedding of desire and passion
The ageing of a heart' s defeat
And then perhaps in time to fashion
From fallacy a fool' s retreat
To where the wooer Death will come
To ravish from his towns of tombs

The Naked Branch

The teachings of the autumn how to shed
The tainted foliage of other springs
The rotting leaves of life that now hang dead
A shake and they would fall and yet one clings

Tenacious to every tiny growth
Each withered hope that once was fresh and green
The human tree that foolishly is loath
To shake its branches free to lie serene

In wait for what the winter months may bring
The courage to despair perhaps presume
That from the autumn ashes there will spring
Of life or death the key to winter's tomb

A Clock Strikes

In the fire
Of desire
Lovers turn
Lovers burn
In the flame

Of their pain
And the stain
Of loves Cain
Turns to shame
And inflame

In the chill
Of the dawn
Love is nil
Lovers yawn

Hostess

The party was a wonderful success
The parting guests of summer all agreed
They paid her compliments with each caress
Then left her with the knowledge of her need

She called the maid the breeze to tidy up
The debris of the gaiety now past
To sweep the grass to empty every cup
To burn the tattered tinsel lightly cast

The golden crowns of leaf the trees had worn
Petaled paper hats that graced the flowers
Frail gaudy streamers from some rainbow torn
Tied the silvered sashes of the showers

Across the setting sun she quickly drew
Pale curtains of grey cloud a blind of mist
Soon loveliness her sorrow would renew
The longing to be loved the need to kiss

She sat within the twilight of her thoughts
That trembled in the twisting grasp of pain
Around her lay the gifts that spring had brought
Decorative desires where love had lain

Optician

The naked eye is weak it hurts to stare
At happiness so so glowing so illumed
The evanescent brightness of its glare
Is searing to the sightof sorrows doomed

Dark spectacles of doubt are duly doomed
To modify the measure of its blaze
And to redeem the minutes lightly pawned
The interest is paid in shadowed days

The images beyond the greenish glass
Are shadows living in a world of shade
Their footsteps are an echo in the past
Their forms appear distorted through a haze

The naked eye is weak and yet to her
Its vision by mutation of the view
It strains the sight and leaves an ugly scar
Dull thickened lens the spectacles renew

Counterfeit

Loved and yet not loving
Why pretend
False happiness
The means unto an end

Sad and yet not crying
Stem the tears
False happiness
Will cover naked years

Laugh there is no laughter
In the eyes
False happiness
Can dim the distant skies

Loved and yet not loving
Better so
False happiness
Will never let him know

Incense

Showers of shrunken leaves
Drifting falling
Fill the waiting arms of the earth
The hours of make—believe

Rain recalling
Gifts that spring bestowed at love's birth
The mad misshapen leaves
Smoulder burning

Sprinkle pale ashes on the grass
Grey swirls upon the breeze
Thoughts are turning
To the fresh and green of the past

The naked branches reach
Pleading crying
To the frowning face of the sky
The taunting breezes screech

Flowers sighing
Open wide their hearts as they die
I have lost love disguised as death
Swiftly creeping

To where clouds are waiting above
Chill is in the breeze's breath
Earth is sleeping
In her dreams of life death is love

The Notebook

The ghosts peer out from every page
Closely barred with words each leaf a cage
Aged ghosts whose youth was never young
In every word are ghosts of ghosts

Whose names must ever be unsung
From every line they peer in hosts
The fragile ghosts of tear stained youth
The adolescent ghosts of age

The tattered talisman of truth
The shrunken symbol of the sage
Pale lovely ghosts of springtime love
Ghosts innumerable immature

Forms mirrored in the clouds above
Frail faery forms whose wings endure
The ghosts of passion and desire
Whose cindered forms in ashes lie

The hectic breeze that fanned the fire
Another ghost if ghosts could die
The ghosts peer out from every page
Close barred with words each leaf a cage

Zoetrope

Deprived of love how swiftly summer wilts
And creeeps into a self created cell
The heady wine of spring is quickly spilt
Its dregs are drunk in some deserted hall

The dregs of bitterness that still retain
Some vestige of the honeyed syrup draught
They truckle through the early autumn rain
Desolate tears of loss where once love laughed

Each fallen leaf with memory is veined
Each broken stalk once held a bloom of dreams
The death of life now leaves the dark earth stained
With scarlet blood that clots in every seam

The rotting raiment of the virgin spring
Is hidden by a tattered cloak of shame
Its gaudy folds around her spent form cling
Her empty arms stretch pleading in their pain

The breeze sweeps past in wild and wanton mood
Swift snatching in his flight her ragged dress
Left naked stripped of every subterfuge
She turns to welcome winter' s harsh caress

The Sculptor

Is there still something left for love to take
Some punishment there yet remains to mete
An automation rotting at the stake
Cannot feel flames that lick around his feet

Is there still one more card for love to play
An ace of anguish hid by times long sleeve
More misery to lengthen every day
In automatons but a brief reprieve

Is there still one more turn loves sword can make
To draw the blood from wounds where there is none
Is there still one more fragment left to break
The shattered heart is slow its pulp is numb

Can love lack pity can love bear to kill
A lifeless corpse who is already dead
Is there no fire whose flames can warm the chill
Or dry the drench of tears despair has shed

Is there still something left for love to give
I close my eyes and wait with bated breath
Is there something left for which to live
Ort must I wait to solve my life with death

Dartry

A boy and a girl both young and both in love
Grey ghosts that haunt my dreams when
I'm awake
This image hides in every star above
Two hearts that beat so fast one had to break

A boy and a girl walk clouded by their dreams
Their hands are touching eyes are all aglow
I look and see the girl that I once seemed
And you you are the boy I use to know

A boy and a girl run laughing through the rain
They stop and kiss and laugh and kiss and so
And life becomes a blue of black and pain
Reality is somewhere long ago

The Crevasse

I tremble on the brink of an incision
Made by the sharp projection of my sin
I tremble with the weight of indecision
The upward crawl the dark defeat within

The mapped out path the various deviations
The short cut to the bottom of the slope
The tampering with tenuous temptations
The cu—de—sac of night no dawn of hope

The backward glance the sorrow sin is mocking
The longing to retrace and to retrieve
Past pebbles from the landslide that is blocking
The way that I have come a soul's reprieve

I lost the way when I could find no reason
Why loneliness and hunger must endure
I chose a way that swiftly led to treason
Betraying the truth the beauty and the pure

I tremble on the brink of an incision
Across from which I see a tiny gate
It's open and beyond there is a vision
I turn away I'm tired it is too late

The Return

I loved I lived I laughed
When life was real
Once long ago
So long ago

I loved I lived I lost
On long ago
The life became a dream an endless dream
Of yesterday

Our yesterday
A dark depressing dream
Just yesterday
A wakeful sleep of death

A dreamless sleep
Of living death
Of deathless death
A sleepless sleep of death

Desired death
The way back through the years
Lost weary years
A long long way

Too long a way
Through wasted weary years
How long the way

Movements

The strange disturbing symphony of night
A subtle symphony of silent sound
Transmitted on the silvered waves of light
The tangled skeins of moon that touch the ground

The soft elusive theme some term it sleep
It trickles through each movement mutely marred
By discords loud with pain that stretches deep
The restless rondo weakens time is passed

The tiny notes of hope despair has drowned
The raucous roaring trumpets of regret
The damning drum beats happiness is ground
The fallen night has lifted now descends
The scenes by sorrow sifted meet and blend

Landscape

The winter sun is cold
Its rays are weak
The winter world is old
Its days are bleak

The winter's light is dark
Without relief
The winter night is stark
And filled with grief

The winter clouds are grey
With icy rain
Death whispers come away
Through clouds of pain

Death whispers come away
Yet I must wait
Oh God I hope and pray
It's not too late

Omega

A careless turn a series of twists
Have bent and almost broken life's frail key
Convulsive jerks a movement in a mist
Unwound this clockwork soon will cease to be

The hands still point to noon though time has fled
The pendulum hangs limp it does not move
The silenced chimes sound only for the dead
That once rang out to welcome life and love

Too late the broken key is now replaced
The rusted mechanism moves in vain
The taut spring breaks behind the passive face
While motionless the hands at noon remain

Nemesis

With diaphonous fingers fog festooned
Through the frosted window pane is peeping
The smouldering shape of the shadowed moon
The only sound is of silent weeping

The street lamp is flickering through the haze
Silvery astral of amber glowing
A huddled form lies in a sleepless daze
The only sound is of sorrow souring

The chapel bell chiming distant and faint
Night ends and the vigil long and weary
Finds no relief as the greying dawn paints
The peeling sky and the sound is dreary

Daedalus

Half way before the middle
The too tight rope has frayed
The clown with trick filled fiddle
He walks and hopes and prays

A sound of distant cheering
Is wafted from below
Unheeding and unhearing
He counts the steps to go

The way that he is facing
So long he' s faint and fears too late to try retracing
The way back through the years

At this point in her notebook, Bernadette lists five more poems in volume two, which is missing.
The title of those five poems are: Elevation; Repetition; The Gift; Itinerant; The Maze

Signposts

I see a long road winding through the May
A path beneath the blossom—laden trees
A white road winding through each golden day
Now chequered by the sun and shadow leaves
I see a long road winding through the May

A path that strays across the distant hills
A sky of blue beneath the clouds of grey
A path that wanders through the mountain rills
I see a long road winding through the May

A path perfumed the sunshine and the rain
The sobbing of the breeze the birdsong gay
A path athwart the sunset s golden flame
I see a long road winding through the tears
That mist above the path and fill the years

Published: Cork Weekly Examiner, June 8, 1957

Retribution

To stand upon the empty beach of dawn
To watch the snake—like silver steep the sands
Beneath the muted echo of the morn
To feel the final pressure of your hands
To watch the grey unbroken sea of day

Stretch to the far horizons of the night
The shining seabiards flying far away
Beyond the fluted fastnesses of light
To clasp the cold and unresponsive dreams
To feel the sharp of sunlight pierce the pain

The early light of gold and silver streams
The morning mists the clouds the splintered rain
Upon the empty beach to stand alone
Like Niobe to feel the creeping stone

Published: Creation, March, 1960

163

Gales

September stirs the sorrow and the heart
Is groping through the twirling swirling leaves
The drifts of gold from swaying branches part
And there is laughter weeping in the breeze

The breeze is brown and wild and warm with rain
The scents are sharp and bitter and the fire
Of scarlet gold is bright and bruised with pain
And there are nights of moon and white desire

The moon the moving shadows and the shades
A surge of coloured madness in the air
The reaching out to grasp before it fades
The stepping back the slumber the despair

Dark dreams distress the ragged wind—torn morn
Desire a crashing echo in the storm

Published: Creation, September, 1960

Dreams and Wishes

Frost fogs the glass and almost hides the stars
That glitter in the blur of Winter blue
The festive sweets are packed in tinselled jars
I dream a dream I wish a wish for you

Bright scarlet holly mocks the mistletoe
The tearing crackers bang the torn masks slip
The tall red candle glistens in the snow
The shadow lovers topple lip to lip

Loud carols ring across the wastes of time
Dark doors are opened splashing out the light
Around the blazing tree the children rhyme
Small angles flit and flutter through the night

The cold starts glitter in the blur of blue
I dream a dream I wish a wish for you

Published: Creation, December, 1960

Round Tables

An article on breakfasts makes her cry
For their were scrambled eggs in Camelot
There were peacocks too and unicorns
And woods where wizards wept
And there was love

Time opens empty rooms now filled with sky
For there were shifting suns in Camelot
There were skys of blue and summer storms
And shores where lovers slept
And there was love

Sun silvers into night above the ruins
For there were many moons in Camelot
There were streets of grey that tumbled stars
On stairs where lovers crept
And there was love

Dawn drifts beyond the distances and dunes
For there were swirling sands in Camelot
Ships at anchor lay and crystal jars
Through seas and shingle swept
And there was love

This poem was probably written in the early 1960s, but is undated

Carnival Times

She remembers a time when she carried each day
Aloft on a string like a coloured balloon
Through streets white with sunlight and over the bridge
Where yellow suns settled and dreamed dreamed at noon
Were borne by the breeze to the rim of the moon

And boats like confetti were crowding the bay
She remembers when nights were as flames on a stem
A blaze in the darkness and dimming the way
Through steets laced in lilac and over the bridge

Where moons made a medly of dreams to delay
Delight of the lovers at ending of day
Making love in the shadows that sheltered them then

This poem was probably written in the early 1960s, but is undated

A Once Upon a Time Time

She remembers Sunday mornings and the afternoons
Making love in the long and narrow room
The endless walks in Hatch Street
And the sound of city bells
A once upon a time time

Once upon a time
Yellow days the coloured awnings and the frame of moons
Naked forms in the shadow light of gloom
The touching and the heartbeat
And the speckled brown of shells
A once upon a time time

Once upon a time
She remembers that strange springtime and the haloed days
The running through the hours to rendezvous
The lying down together
And the changing squares of sky
A once upon a time time

Once upon a time
April carnivalled in sunshine and the sword was raised
Mask upon mask the silhouettes withdrew
Their faces lost forever
Miming whispers and a cry
A once upon a time time

Once upon a time

Published: Social & Personal, July, 1986

Flower Window

Troubador dust on yellow stone
The smell of cotton in a summer town
Of castled hills and broken amphorae
The honey spills beyond the distant bay

The shapes are blurring and blending they drown
Above the clouds of dream are blown
The petals pile on polished wood
Pale figures in the landscape of a room

Crumble in the motes of the changing light
A colour of carnations in the night
The scent of lilac lingers in the gloom
Lace tracery on seas of mud

Thin sunlight glints on metal grids
Strange horned sheep are huddled as they graze
And gaze beyond the winding moorland road
The inn dog sleeps and dreams of prince and toad

The night falls and the moon a golden glaze
Gleams on the rooftop pyramids
Behind the rainbow coloured glass
The fantasies of water rise and fall

And love remains a prism in the mind
The sharp and shining brilliance blends and blinds
And brings again a time beyond recall
Two shadows lengthen on the grass

Published: IT magazine, October, 1982

Pink Tulips

The star crossed lovers had scrambled eggs for breakfast before they went their
separate ways
He to a slow and lingering life
She to a strange miscelleny of moons
The days of yellow suns in rented rooms

Shards of antique glass the surgeon' s knife
Jigsaw in the aftermath the days
To souls extinction honey dregs the rising gas
Flowers for the lady the flower—seller cried

She carried them through Customs to the plane
At the airport she had nothing to declare
Life was static as she hurtled through the air
To find the open places of her pain
There were pills to keep her living as she died

Published: The Irish Times, March 19, 1983

The poems, above, are in chronological order, as Bernadette wrote them in her poetry notebook, with
all her spellings and lack of punctuation exactly as she wrote. The more recent poems in the above
collection were all published, with date and place of publication indicated.

In the early 1950s, she wrote a number of poems in Old Irish, which has been translated into modern Irish and English by Ellen Monnelly.

Oiche Deire Fomhair

A night in October
Oiche chorruighuil
An odd night
Is ceannta
Ag déanamh baoth cainnte
Making foolish talk
Gan Leiriú
Without showing
Asg déabamh grádh
Making love
Gan toradh
Without result
Oiche mí—suaimhneach
An uneasy night
Gan coladh
Without sleep
Ag iarriadh eálód
Trying to escape

Ón smaointe
From the thoughts
Ag iarriadh eálód
Trying to escape
Ón saol
From Life
Maidin
Morning
Gan faoisimh
Without relief
Ag féachaint ar aghaidh
Go?
To . . .
Ag feiscint
Seeing
Tada
Nothing

Is tú mo grá

You are my love
Is tú mo grá
You are my love
Anoise is coiche
Now and forever
Anseo lion féin
Here by myself
Is cuimhin liom cráit
I remember . . . .
Bhí an ré is na réalta ag lonnrad
The king and the stars were shining
Suas ins an spéir geal
Up in the bright sky
Nuair a blaiseesas do beola is . . .
When I tasted your lips and . . .
Mé fá draoicht do réior
And fell under a spell because of it
Bhí do súil nar a . . .
Your eyes were . . . .
Lasaid meallta?
Ar mo croí buail do croí
On my heart beat your heart
Go láidir mear
Strongly and quickly

Bhí do poga so—blasta mar an druaic. A uileann san farraig
Your kiss was very tasty like that in the sea
Cuir tú smaoimim? Ar mo croí is
You put on my heart and
Anois táimm fé geasa an grá
San gan lá
A life without days
Oiche de síor
A constant night
Saol fé sgai?
A life under . . .
Ag féachaint siar
Looking back
I? grádh
Falling in love
Saol gain riar
A life without rules
Saol gan lá
A life without days
Oiche de síor
A constant night

Smaoineamh

Thinking
Toradh an grádh
The result of loving
Ba cúis le mo cás
Is my reason for living
Toradh an grádh
The result of loving
Ba cúis le mo bás
Is the cause of my death

Tup (?)

Saol gan saol
A life without life
'sead saol gan tú'
Is a life without without you
Gan scaipeadh géal
Without the spreading of light
Saol gan tnú
A life without excitement
Gnó gan céill
Business without sense
Saol gab fíu
A life not worth living
Saol gan saol
A life without life
'sead saol gan tú
Is a life without you
Saol gan fáth
A life without purpose
'sead saol gan grá
Is a life lacking love gan neart (?) without strength (?)
Saol gan beart
A life without measure
Tada romaim
Nothing ahead of me
Saol fé brón
A life under sadness
Saol gan fátth
Life without purpose
'Sead saol gan grá
Is a life without love

Easpa

Absence
Liaisas agus uaigneas
(?) And loneliness
An saol gan grá
Life is without love
Liaias us mí-shuaimhneas
(?) and discomfort
De síor am crádadh
Constant torment

An aimsear (?) cailte

The weather's lost
Teangmháil ár mbéal
The language of our mouths
Na huaireanna oil-daite
The multi—coloured hours
Gan easpa béal
With no mouth lacking

Dorchadas na hoíche

The darkness of night
An saol gan beart
A life without measure
Mar sop on agóid na gaoithe (?)
Briste gan beart
Broken without measure

Aiteas (?) Grá

? of love

Aoibheas croí

The heart' s joy
Ansin díomá
And then disappointment
Gan aon faoi
Without any (?)
Béal le béal
Mouth to mouth
Croí le croí
Heart to heart
Níl ann ach seal
Nothing there but space
Seal suirghe
(?) space
Saol gan saol
Life without life
Saol gan léiriú
Life without showing
Gnó gan chéill
Senseless business
Briseadh croí
Heartbreak

Casadh

Turn
Tháinigh tú im treo
You came my way
Is mé ag suibial aréir
When I was (?) last night
Theas tú os mo chomhair
You stood in front of me
Samaoinigh mé go soiléir
I remember it clearly
Ar an oíche deire fómhair
On that night in October
Ar ha hoicheanna go léir
On all of the nights
Ar an gliondar is an gleó
The joy and the glow
Is an leriseadh croí dá réir
And the heart' s display
Nuair a tháninigh tú im treo
When you came my way
Aréir
Last night

An Oíche Fáda

The long night
Is fada an oíche
The night is long
Is mé gan coladh
And I have not slept
Ar iarraudh í mealladh
I'm trying to entice it
Mealladh gan toradh
But with no luck
Is fada an oíche
The night is long
Is mé gain cosaint
And I have no defence
Ó lionnsaige mo smoainte
From those attacking my thoughts
Gan fiú sos sroisint
Without stopping
Is fada an oíche
The night is long
Is mé gain réidhteach
An I have no solution
Ar fáth mo bhuadharta

As to the reason for my worries
(?) Lúi ag éisteacht
(?) Lying, listening
Le fuaimeanna aite
To the strange sounds
Trí cuimhneas na hóiche
Through the silence of the night
Le h—uaigneas is fathcíos
To loneliness and?
Tré readighil na goaithe
Through the wind
Is fada an oíche
The night is long
Fada gan coladh
Long and without sleep
In aisce mo smaointe
Free from my thoughts
In aisce gan toradh
Free without results

Published Rosc, October/ November 1953

An Féadair

It can
Chuas I bhfolac ón saol
I went hiding from life
Ach tháinigh sé im lorg
But it came looking for me
Diúltaigheas don tsaol
(?) to the life
Is d' imigh m gan imairg
And it left without me
Do dheineas iarraidh eálódh
I did try to escape
Thuas ar bharr an tslébhe
I went to the top of the mountain
Thuas I bhfad ón gleó
I went far from the glow
Measc am ailinn is an fhreaoigh
The beauty and the . . . .
Do dhieineas iarraidh eálódh
I did try to escape
Ach ní fhuair mé sásamh ceart
But I didn' t get what I wanted

Bhí rud éígin in easnamh
Something was missing
Teipeadh ar mo bheart
My action failed
Do chuas ar tóir an saoil
I went on a life journey
'S thuille níor diúltaigheas dó
And over all . . . .
Ach is measa bo chas anois
My situation is worse now
'nfheadair an fear éalódh
Maybe it's better to escape

Published Rosc July 1953

Gluaiseachtaí

Movements
Gluaseacht mall an rinnce
The slow movements of dancing
Fuaimeanna draochta an cheóil
The magical sound of music
Mothaím, cloisim
I feel, I hear
Go fóil
Still
Gluaiseacht mear na hoíche
The quick movements of night
Scaramains I leatrh sholas an lae
In the half—light of day
Leath sola liach
The grey hald—light
An lae
Of day
Gluaiseacht siar no smaointe
The backward movements of my thoughts
Siar ar na h—eachraí atá thar
Over the things that have happened
Is mé I'm aonair
And me on my own
Gan beart
Without action

Bernadette's life story

Foreword and acknowledgements

This is the story of my dear and greatly beloved wife, Bernadette, and her family, as well her own life story and career, all of which was spent in what is now the Department of Foreign Affairs and Trade. Bernadette and I first met in 1970, a meeting that was pure chance, since one of Bernadette's colleagues, who should have been the one to meet me, the inquiring journalist, but who was on a long phone conversation and asked Bernadette to do the needful.

We started doing a line almost immediately and within less than two years, were married. Bernadette has been doing the needful ever since, a loving and always supportive wife, who has always given me great support in my career, especially with all the books I've written or contributed to, so far numbering 80. These days, Bernadette's health has deteriorated and she is no longer living at home, but in St Mary's Home in Pembroke Park, Ballsbridge, where I go to see her every day.

This book is a tribute to Bernadette and her many talents, especially her poetic talents. She is a wonderful woman and this book is my way of acknowledging the often hectic but always rich legacy of our years together.

I should also like to thank the people who've helped in the production of this book, including her sister, Gloria Williams. Clare Bohan, based at Templemore in Co Tipperary has been an immense help in tracing Bernadette's genealogical connections in Thurles, through her father's side of the family and indeed in Dublin. Tommie Griffin, a distant relative of Bernadette's in Thurles, has also been of much assistance. I also appreciate the help of Lynn Brady, genealogical researcher at the Glasnevin Trust in Dublin and Dominic Butler, assistant curator at the Lancashire Infantry Museum in Preston, Lancashire, England, for his help in tracing details of Bernadette's maternal grandfather, Michael Tuohey, who was killed in action during the first world war. I'd also like to thank Dean Lochner of the Bondi Group in Ballsbridge, Dublin, for all his technical assistance and Hackett Digital, Lower Baggot Street, Dublin, for all their imaging help.

I am especially indebted to Ellen Monnelly for her help in translating the poems that Bernadette wrote in the early 1950s in Old Irish; Ellen translated them most graciously into modern Irish and English. Aisling Curley, Thelma Byrne, Maria Gillen and Mary J. Murphy, have also given me much encouragement along the way, as the book progressed.

Bernadette Oram, born Bernadette Quinn—her family story

Bernadette was born on March 4, 1930, at Number 6, Dean Street, in the Liberties district of Dublin. Her father, Hugh, was a train examiner for the Great Southern Railways, while her mother Mary, usually known as May, was a homemaker.

At that stage, home for the Quinn family was a flat above Williams' grocery shop in Dean Street. That grocery shop had been there for many years; it was listed by Thom's Directory as early as 1905. But by 1937, it had changed hands and was trading as Malone & Browne's grocery shop.

Her father, Hugh, and her mother, Mary, had got married on June 4, 1928, at the church of St Nicholas of Myra, just round the corner in Francis Street. When they got married, they were both described as living at Number 6, Dean Street.

Hugh had been born in Dublin into a family with long connections with Thurles, Co Tipperary. His father, Kevin, had been an engine driver, although in the 1911 census, he was described as a labourer. Kevin had married Alice Connors in Thurles in 1890; Kevin's father, also called Kevin, was injured in a work accident on the railway, in Thurles, and died after two days in the workhouse in Thurles, on October 20, 1892, at the age of 70. A much earlier ancestor of Bernadette's had been active in the White Quakers in Dublin in the earlier part of the 19th century.

After Kevin and Alice married, they lived at Garravocleheen, which has various spellings, and Bohernave, in Thurles, before moving to Dublin.

Kevin Quinn, Hugh's father, and Alice, Hugh's mother, eventually moved to Dublin, after four of their six children had been born in Thurles. In Dublin, the family lived at Number 12, Richmond Cottages, Emmet Road, Inchicore. Hugh was their second youngest child, although dates differ as to what year he was born. The 1911 census says he was eight at the time, which would have meant that he had been born in 1903, but in his family, it was accepted that he had been born in 1902, the date given on his gravestone.

The youngest child was Mary Ellen, a year younger than her brother Hugh. Both Mary Ellen and Hugh were born in Dublin. Mary Ellen went on to marry and have a large family, but died at a relatively young age.

Residents of a house 12 in Richmond Cottages (New Kilmainham, Dublin)

Show all information

Surname	Forename	Age	Sex	Relation to head	Religion	Birthplace	Occupation	Literacy	Irish Language	Marital Status	Specified Illnesses	Years Married	Children Born	Children Living
Quinn	Kevin	48	Male	Head of Family	R C	Tipperary	Labourer	Read and write	English	Married			6	
Quinn	Alice	39	Female	Wife	R C	Tipperary	-	Read and write	English	Married		18	6	6
Quinn	James Jos	17	Male	Son	R C	Tipperary	Messenger	Read and write	English	Single				
Quinn	Kevin	16	Male	Son	R C	Tipperary	Messenger	Read and write	English	Single				
Quinn	Henry Patrick	15	Male	Son	R C	Tipperary	Messenger	Read and write	Irish and English	Single				
Quinn	Annie Mary	11	Female	Daughter	R C	Tipperary	Messenger	Read and write	English	Single				
Quinn	Hugh	8	Male	Son	R C	Dublin		Read and write	English					
Quinn	Mary Ellen	7	Female	Daughter	R C	Dublin			English					
Connors	Michael	38	Male	Boarder	R C	Tipperary	Labourer	Read and write	English	Single				

The residents of Richmond Cottages, Emmet Road, Inchicore-Hugh Quinn, his brothers and sisters, mother and father and his mother's brother, from the 1911 census.

In the 1911 census, four of the children children, James (17), Kevin (16), Henry Patrick (15) and Annie Mary (11) were all listed as messengers. They had all been born in Thurles, with Annie Mary the last of the family born there. Of Hugh Quinn's five siblings, Bernadette was most aware of two of them, Kevin, the second oldest son, and Henry Patrick, the third oldest son. Kevin followed in his father's footsteps and went to work on the railway for his entire working life. He was a very gruff man and Bernadette never took to him; he also had a lifelong preference for whiskey. Kevin's first wife was Mary Price, whom he married at Goldenbridge church in 1921; she died young and he subsequently remarried.

The third oldest son of Kevin and Alice Quinn was totally different, fondly remembered as Uncle Henry. He too went to work on the railways, but in an administrative role. He was a very quiet, well mannered and diligent man, who never married. He had a great interest in books and amassed a considerable library. He was also very keen on horse riding, which in those days was a sport rarely enjoyed by anyone outside the aristocracy. He lived at home, with his mother, after his father had died, but tragically, at an early age, around 40, he contracted TB, then a fatal illness and he died at home, in his mother's arms.

The family home at Richmond Cottages had one other resident at the time of the 1911 census, Michael Connors, aged 38, also a native of Thurles and described as a labourer. He was a year younger than Kevin Quinn's wife Alice and presumably a brother of Alice, since they shared the same family name, Connors.

By 1920, Kevin Quinn and his wife Alice had moved from Emmet Road to Number 4, Phoenix Street, also in Inchicore. This area of Inchicore, off Sarsfield Road, is known locally as 'The Ranch'; Phoenix Street was and is an enclave of 50 small houses. It was often said within the family that Kevin Quinn had died from injuries received while taking part in the 1916 Easter Rising, but in 1928, when one of his younger children, Hugh, got married, Kevin Quinn was still alive, aged 65.

When Bernadette's father, Hugh, was growing up, he went to the Model School in Inchicore, a short distance from the family home. Hugh often related how the headmaster was a man called T. P. Murray, who had seen good potential in the young lad. Murray, who was born at Macroom, Co Cork, also became noted as a playwright of considerable stature, writing nearly 20 plays.

Yet despite the considerable success of some of his plays at the Abbey Theatre, he didn't retire from teaching until 1932, when he went to live in quiet retirement at Sandymount Avenue, Dublin.

As soon as Hugh was of an age to start work, 14, he followed his father and his grandfather into the railways. Hugh would have started with the Great Southern Railway in Inchicore in the middle of the first world war, in all probability during the fateful year of 1916. It wasn't until the mid—1920s that all the railways in this part of Ireland were amalgamated into Great Southern Railways. A further 20 years on, the railways became part of CIE, set up in 1945 and nationalised in 1950.

But from an early age, Hugh had a great love of music, which he retained all his life. During the latter part of the War of Independence (1919—1921), he had a remarkable and at the time, terrifying, experience. He would have been 17 or 18 at the time.

He had been playing in a local concert in Inchicore one evening and afterwards, was walking home, carrying his violin in his case. A lorry pulled up beside him, some Black and Tans jumped out and ordered him to get in the back of the lorry. During the time that the Black and Tans were active in Ireland, many people picked up by them in that manner often met a brutal death, regardless of whether or not they had any republican connections.

Hugh Quinn was absolutely terrified that he was going to meet the same fate, but then the Black and Tan soldiers told him they were having a party that night at their barracks and wanted someone to play for them. Hugh played for hours, as if his life depended upon it, which it did, and at the end of the party, he was simply told he was free to go home.

Bernadette's mother, Mary, came from the Touhey family, also resident in the Liberties, but whose connections went back to Limerick. Throughout the 19th century, Limerick had a pig processing industry, which explains why Mary's father and her mother's father, were both pork butchers.

Michael Tuohey, Mary's father, married Elizabeth McGrath, on October 22, 1905, at the church of St Nicholas of Myra in Francis Street, the same church where their daughter Mary married Hugh Quinn on June 4, 1928. At the date of the marriage, Michael was recorded as living at 7 Christchurch Place, while Elizabeth was recorded as living at 59 Francis Street. Mary Touhey, Bernadette's mother, was born on November 17, 1906, when the family was living at Number 99 Francis Street. Two years later, the Touheys moved to 24 Patrick Street.

Michael had been born in 1885. Although a pork butcher by trade, he joined the British Army at an early age, and was listed as having taken part in the South African campaign, against the Boers, in 1901. He had enlisted in Dublin, in the Ist battalion of the East Lancashire Regiment and then went on to fight on the Allied side in the First World War. He became a sergeant and was killed in France on May 14, 1915. At the time of his death, he was listed as being husband of Elizabeth and resident at Number 6, Dean Street, Dublin, the family home where Bernadette was born 15 years later, in 1930. Michael is listed on panel 34 of the Menin Gate memorial at Ypres in present day Belgium. In July, 1919, after the war had ended, his widow, Elizabeth, was granted an annuity of £8.

TOUHEY, MICHAEL. Reg. No. 5868. Rank, Sergeant, The East Lancashire Regiment, 1st Batt.; killed in action, France, May 14, 1915; born Dublin.

Michael Tuohey, Bernadette's maternal grandfather, who was killed in action in 1915, during the first world war. From: Ireland's Memorial Records.

When Bernadette was a young child, any discussion in the family home about what were loosely referred to as "the authorities" was swiftly terminated by Bernadette's mother or grandmother, Elizabeth, saying that they didn't want to lose the widow's pension granted to Elizabeth.

Strangely, while Bernadette and her immediate family had a long relationship with Bernadette's maternal grandmother, Elizabeth, for the simple reason that she lived at home with Bernadette and her family for many years. Yet the connections to Limerick of her late husband, Michael, killed in the first world war, always remained shadowy. On the other hand, Bernadette's paternal grandparents, Kevin and Alice, were much better documented. Yet Gloria, Bernadette's sister, has no recollections of meeting her paternal grandfather, Kevin, and only a few memories of meeting her paternal grandmother, Alice, when she, Gloria, was still very young. At that stage, Alice was dressed in black, widow's weeds, while Gloria also remembers that she was an extremely good cook. At the time that Hugh and Mary got married, Hugh's parents were still alive; his father, Kevin, was 65 in 1928.

Before Bernadette's parents got married, in 1928, her mother, Mary, was noted for being a good looking woman with big brown eyes and a gentle manner. She always had a great knack for getting on with people and there were reportedly several suitors before she decided to tie the knot with her husband, Hugh, in 1928. As a young woman, before she married, Mary worked in a number of shop jobs, most prominently in the Gramophone Shop in Johnson's Court, which runs from Grafton Street, alongside the church in Clarendon Street. The Gramophone Shop was in fact HMV's first shop venture in Dublin and was noted for its wide selection of 78 rpm gramophone records. It stayed open until 9pm each night and potential customers were told to look out for the electric sign outside, quite a novelty in those days. It's quite possible, although unproven, that Hugh Quinn's love of music brought him to the Gramophone Shop, where he met the attractive looking young woman behind the counter.

Marriage No. 84 Registered by me, this 38th day of July 1928 Keith Blanche Registrar.	1928. Marriage solemnized at the Roman Catholic Church of St Nicholas in the Registrar's District of No. 3 South City in the Union of Dublin in the County of the City of Dublin							
No. (1)	When Married. (2)	Name and Surname. (3)	Age. (4)	Condition. (5)	Rank or Profession. (6)	Residence at the Time of Marriage (7)	Father's Name and Surname. (8)	Rank or Profession of Father. (9)
84	4th June 1928	Hugh Quinn	Full	Bachelor	Tram Examiner	6 Dean St	Kevin Quinn	Engine Driver
		Mary Tuohy	Full	Spinster	—	6 Dean St	Michael Tuohy	Pork Butcher

Married in the Roman Catholic Chapel of St Nicholas according to the Rites and Ceremonies of the Roman Catholic Church by me, Francis J Dunlea CC

This Marriage was solemnized between us,	Hugh M J Quinn	in the Presence of us,	Michael Tuohy
	Mary Tuohy		Mary Quinn

Marriage certificate for Hugh and Mary (May) Quinn, Bernadette's parents, who were married at St Nicholas of Myra church in Francis Street, Dublin, in 1928.

After they got married, they spent their honeymoon on the Isle of Man; in those days, it was very unusual for anyone outside wealthy families to travel outside Ireland for holidays or honeymoons. Many years later, after Bernadette had married Hugh Oram, they quite often returned to the Isle of Man and on two occasions, were accompanied by Bernadette's parents, Hugh and Mary.

Well before Hugh Quinn got married, two of his siblings had done likewise. One of his older brothers, James, had married Julia Flanagan in the church at Chapelizod on October 10, 1920, while the following year, on April 27, 1921, another older brother, Kevin, had married Mary Price, at the church in Goldenbridge, not far from the Quinn family home.

After Bernadette's birth, the family was on the move. About 1932, they moved to The Crescent in Marino,

Kelly's Corner, Dublin. The Quinn family lived here from the mid-1930s until the early 1950s; their house at Number 8 Upper Camden Street was just to the right of Brady's chemist's shop. Photo:archiseek

probably Number 23, because this was the only house in The Crescent that was divided into flats. But Bernadette's father, Hugh, being a true southsider, hated every minute of living north of the River Liffey and often told me that he couldn' t wait to get back to the "right" side of the river. A short time there, the family, Hugh and Mary Quinn with their infant daughter Bernadette, moved to accommodation at Number 8, Upper Camden Street, close to the junction with Harcourt Street and the start of the South Circular Road.

The present day façade of Number 8 Upper Camden Street, the house where the Quinn family lived from the mid-1930s until the early 1950s. Photo:Hugh Oram

It was here in 1935 that Bernadette's younger sister, Gloria, was born. Before Bernadette came along, Hugh and Mary had a son who was sadly stillborn. When Gloria was born, she was quite a large baby; in those days, it was usually the case for births to take place at home. Bernadette has often recalled that while Gloria was being born, her father was in such a nervous frame of mind that he went out to the back garden and spent the time cutting glass!

When the two children, Bernadette and Gloria, were young, their mother and their grandmother often took them in summer to such places as Herbert Park, which was within reasonable walking distance. Bernadette remembers that first, they went to the old Johnston, Mooney & O' Brien shop in Ballsbridge—where the Herbert Park Hotel is now situated—to stock up on bread and cakes for their picnics in the park. Later on, when the two girls were teenagers, they went further afield, taking the bus to Rathfarnham and then walking as far as the Hell Fire Club and beyond. On one occasion, such was their predeliction for walking, the two of them walked home all the way from Dún Laoghaire.

Bernadette's grandmother, Elizabeth, continued to live with the family. From time to time, her grandfather' s medals, from his time in the East Lancashire Regiment, were brought out, to be shown around, although Bernadette' s mother never liked being reminded of them. To the end of her life, she considered that there were no good Germans, as they had been responsible for the death of her father.

Apart from his work on the railways, Bernadette' s father, Hugh, continued with his music making. In the 1930s, before the second world war, he had his own band, the Quintonians. Bernadette remembers vividly that one of the band members worked in the old Jacob' s biscuit factory in Bishop Street, Dublin, and that every Friday night, he' d bring her a present of a pack of broken biscuits from Jacob' s. In the 1950s and 1960s, Hugh continued his music making, including as a lead violinist with the Nell Kane Orchestra.

Nell was a remarkable woman, born in Wicklow town, who spent many years living in Dublin and who returned to her home town for the last 30 years of her life. She died in March, 2016, at the age of 98.

For many years, she ran her own orchestra, which often played to raise money for charities. Hugh was a close friend of Nell' s and one of the key players. Bernadette remembers one famous occasion when the orchestra was playing in the College of Surgeons in Dublin when one of the strings on her father' s violin broke and he stormed off the stage in disgust.

In the 1930s, Hugh' s mentor in the Great Southern Railways was a man called Joe Reynolds, who had a more senior position in the company. Hugh taught him to play the violin and they became great friends, a friendship that endured for many years. Joe on one occasion offered Hugh promotion to a much more comfortable indoor job with the railway company, but he declined, perferring to remain a train examiner.

The exterior of Harcourt Street station, which closed down in 1959; it was very familiar to Bernadette and she and her family often took the train from here to Bray. Photo:Hugh Oram

One of the places where Bernadette's father worked for several years was the railway station to Bray and Bernadette has vivid memories of family trips out to Bray, where they were warmly greeted by Hugh's colleagues. Those trips to Bray started from the old Harcourt Street station, very close to the Quinn family home in Upper Camden Street. Much later on, after Bernadette had got married in 1972, an elderly Joe Reynolds wrote to her several times and said that he hoped to come and meet her again, with her new husband, Hugh, but sadly, this promise never materialised.

Even nearer the family home, in fact literally just round the corner, was a remarkable family—owned shop that's still going strong today. Brady's chemists shop had opened in 1894 and is still owned by the Bradys today; one of the Bradys was Philip Brady, who was made Lord Mayor of Dublin in 1960. Bernadette often met him at official functions; he had a remarkable life, dying in 1995 in his 102nd year. When Bernadette was a child, if she ever suffered from childish ailments, she just went to Bradys round the corner, although on one memorable occasion, she had to go to the old Childrens' Hospital in Harcourt Street. One of Philip Brady's children, Gerard, became a well—known optician and also had a long spell as a TD; both of us got to know Gerard very well.

Elizabeth always had poor health and in February, 1947, she died from a heart attack at the family home in Upper Camden Street. Bernadette has often told me that the death of her grandmother came in the middle of the big winter freeze—up of 1947, when Ireland had what was probably the worst winter of the 20th century. Bernadette has often recalled how they had to traipse through the snow to get to relatives and tell them the sad news, because they had no phone, while the funeral procession to Glasnevin cemetery was a horrendous experience, because the roads

Interior of Harcourt Street railway station, Dublin. It was close to the Quinn family home in Upper Camden Street and the Quinns often travelled from here to Bray for a day out. The station closed in 1959.
Photo: The Harcourt Street Line by Brian Mac Aongusa

Woolworth's old store at the top of Grafton Street, Dublin. When Bernadette was a child, she was often taken to the café there for a treat.

and pavements were piled high with snow and ice. Elizabeth Touhey, Bernadette' s maternal grandmother, was laid to rest in grave number DF64 in the St Paul' s section of the vast Glasnevin cemetery. She was buried in a grave owned by her sister, Mary McGrath.

After the death of Elizabeth Tuohey, Hugh and Mary Quinn and their two daughters stayed in the house at Upper Camden Street for only a few years more. The Irish Industrial Benefit Building Society founded in 1873, was for many years located at Number 6, Upper Camden Street; much later, it changed its name to the Irish Nationwide Building Society, which eventually collapsed during the great economic crash that started in 2008, with debts of close to €6 billion. But in the early 1950s, the building society was in expansionist mode and wanted to expand its premises to include Number 8, Upper Camden Street, which it owned.

One of the advantages of living in Upper Camden Street, apart from the fact it was so close to the city centre and to the Department where Bernadette worked, was that it was within easy walking distance of the old Harcourt Street station, which closed down in 1959. Before that however, it was regularly used by the family to take the train out to Bray. For a number of years, Hugh was stationed at Bray station so that anytime the Quinn family arrived there, they always got a warm welcome.

Two offers of alternative housing were made to the Quinn family. One offer was of a house at South Hill, Dartry, but this was rejected for various reasons, including the fact that it was so far from Hugh Quinn' s work on the railways at Inchicore. The second offer was accepted, a terrace house in a cul de sac that was then being constructed in Rialto, much nearer to Inchicore. Number 2 Rialto Drive became the new family home.

On one side, at Number 1, lived William Mitchell; after his death, his widow continued to live there. On the other side, at Number 3, were Tom and Anne O' Neill, who remained close friends of the Quinn family for many years. Sometimes, Hugh and Mary went on holidays with the O' Neills. By the time the Quinn family had moved to Rialto Drive, Bernadette had been working in the Department of External Affairs for about five years. Her younger sister, Gloria, worked for Dublin Corporation and for civil defence. At one stage, Gloria was working in the sewers department at the Corporation and on one memorable occasion, when Mary Quinn was asked how her daughters were doing, she replied that one, Bernadette, was in the foreign service, all very glamorous, while the other, Gloria, was in sewers.

Bernadette's father, Hugh, continued to work for CIE, which had taken over Great Southern Railways in 1945, and stayed their until he retired in 1968, ending the long Quinn family connection with the railways. Hugh Quinn died in December, 1988, at the age of 86. His widow, Mary, continued to live in the house for about 18 months, but her health deteriorated so much that she had to be transferred to Bru Chaoimhin in Cork Street, an old persons' residence run by what was then the Eastern Health Board. It had been built in the early 19th century as a workhouse and fever hospital. Mary spent nine years there and died in July, 1997, at the age of 91. She is buried with her husband, Hugh, at St Fintan' s cemetery, Sutton, on the northside of Dublin. Bernadette and her husband, Hugh, have both expressed their wish, in Hugh' s will, to be buried in the same grave.

Gloria, who had got married not long before Bernadette, continued to live in the district with her husband, Eamonn, a lecturer at Kevin Street college, part of the Dublin Institute of Technology. They lived on the South Circular Road, before moving to a house near the old Montrose Hotel on the Stillorgan Road and then, finally, to Dartry Park. Eamonn, a much loved person with a great, mischievous sense of humour, died in 2005.

Bernadette continued to live at home in Rialto Drive until she and Hugh married in June, 1972.

Bernadette's Thurles connections

Within Bernadette's family, her mother's connections with Limerick where downplayed; as her mother's parents had long been resident in Dublin, but her father's connections with Thurles, Co Tipperary, were more dominant. Indeed, when Bernadette and her sister Gloria were teenagers, they often went to stay with relatives in Thurles, where they were often joined for shorter breaks by their father, Hugh, and their mother, Mary or May.

They stayed with the Griffins in Thurles. Tommy Griffin had married into the extended Quinn family from the town. Tommy had spent much of his younger life in America, where he did well and amassed substantial wealth. On one of his last trips home from America, before he returned to Ireland for good, he was staying in Hayes Hotel, Thurles (where the Gaelic Athletic Association had been founded in 1884).

At dinner in the hotel on the last night before he set sail for America, he got into conversation with the hotel manageress, Bridie Quinn. She noticed that he had a lot of money in his wallet and offered to keep it overnight in the hotel safe. Tommy told her that he was going back to America to start tidying up his affairs there, but that he intended to return to Ireland in the near future, for good. He also told her that when he got back, he would marry her. Tommy was as good as his word and when he returned, he and Bridie did get married. Well before that had happened, Tommy's father, Maurice, had also married into the Quinn family in 1873, when he he married Mary Anne Quinn in Littleton, Co Tipperary.

Tommy set up a butcher's shop at Parnell Street, in the centre of Thurles, and given his aptitude for business, it did well. Bernadette and Gloria often stayed at the Griffin family home in Thurles, which Gloria now remembers as being a cut above other local houses, spacious with an upstairs gallery. She also remembers that the Griffins were so well—known in Thurles, that when they went into local

Griffin's shop in Parnell Street, Thurles, Co Tipperary. Bridie and her husband Tommy are centre and right. When Bernadette and her sister Gloria were teenagers, they often went for holidays to stay with the Griffins in Thurles, who were related to their father, Hugh. Photo: Tommie Griffin

sweet shops, they weren't asked to pay and when they were in groups that went to the town cinema, they were given the best seats and not asked to pay until the performance was over.

For many years, Hugh Quinn, Bernadette's father, often said that the family had blue blood in their veins. Hugh had a great sense of humour and a certain love of divilment, so that these remarks were often dismissed as just another of Hugh's jokes. But in fact they had their basis in solid genealogical fact.

A large scale farmer who lived just outside Thurles, Nason Crone, had a number of daughters and one of them, Alice, married Bernadette's grandfather, Kevin Quinn. The Crones were part of the landed gentry who for so many years were a key element of life in the small north Co Cork town of Doneraile. But Nason Crone left Doneraile and went on to own substantial holdings of farm land near Thurles. He lived in a place called Annsgrove, not far from Thurles, and died on November 20, 1861. Nason had a son

Byblox House, Doneraile, Co Cork. The Quinns of Thurles were related to the Crones, who lived in Bylbox House, by marriage.

called Bernard, who became a shopkeeper in Cashel; he married Eliza O'Reilly in the Catholic church there in 1879.

The Crones were closely connected to the Doneraile branch of the Synan family, who were of Welsh origin and who came to Ireland with Strongbow at the time of the Anglo—Norman invasion of Ireland in the late 12th century. Between the 13th and 15th centuries, the Synans were very powerful in Doneraile, but eventually faded out. As for the Crone connection in Doneraile, this can be traced back to 1793 when Robert Crone bought the townland of Byblox just outside Doneraile and built Byblox House, a very large three storey mansion. Robert's son, Major John Crone, made Byblox famous in the 19th century for the extravagant hunt balls and all night parties in the mansion. The Crone connection with Doneraile lasted until 1902.

At that stage, the house was occupied by Jane Crone, who had married her cousin, William Croker, who had died young. Then she lost her only son in one of the Boer Wars in southern Africa; he was just 19. Seven years after his death, she sold the house and the estate, in 1902, to a man called Eustace Morrough—Bernard and moved to Limerick. That severed the Crone connection with Doneraile. Eventually, in the mid—1960s, the great house just outside Doneraile was demolished by the then German owner of the estate. A more modern house was built in its place and it's still there today, owned by Marguerite Dwan and offering upmarket bed and breakfast accommodation. Only the garden walls and some outbuildings from the original Byblox House still remain.

So the Griffin and Quinn families in Thurles had intermarried and the Quinns had formed a connection to the Crone family. The Quinn family had a long connection with Thurles; the father of Kevin Quinn, Bernadette's grandfather, was also called Kevin and also worked on the railways. He was the man killed in an accident on the railway at Thurles in 1890. Bernadette's father, Hugh, was the fourth generation of Quinns to have worked on the railway, with the first three having done that in Thurles. The railway station at Thurles had been opened in 1848, which meant that the Quinns had close on 120 years' connection with the railways, up until the retirement of Bernadette's father, Hugh, from CIE in 1968. The Quinns in Thurles lived in a highly populated area called Garryvideheen, close to Bohernanave, not far from the railway station. Today, in this same area can be found Semple Stadium.

As for Tommy Griffin and his family, after he retired from business, the butcher's shop closed down and became part of the family living quarters. One of the children of Tommy and his wife Alice was a son Tommie, who became a well—known solicitor and who died in 2014.

He was survived by his sisters Mai and Bridie. Another member of the extended Griffin family in Thurles was Lt Col Jack Griffin, whose family home was at Clongour, Thurles. He had been in the Defence Forces for 29 years and was home on leave from Brussels in October, 2015, when he was killed by a car while out jogging on the Horse and Jockey Road very close to Thurles. Married in 2005, he left a wife and three young children.

Apart from her connections with Thurles as a teenager, Bernadette visited the then quiet thatched cottage village of Adare in Co Limerick, which she found fascinating because of its rural quaintness. These days, Adare is jam packed with traffic and tourists, a completely different scene altogether.

Cottage in Adare, Co Limerick. When Bernadette was a teenage, she stayed in Adare on several occasions; it was then a quiet country village, full of thatched cottages, but these days, is choked with traffic. Photo: Bygone Limerick by Hugh Oram

Bernadette's career in the foreign service

B ernadette showed signs of considerable intelligence at an early age. When the family was still living at Upper Camden Street, and Bernadette was still at pre—school age, she went to a kindergarten on the South Circular Road.

One of her earliest memories was of her mother taking herself and her sister to Herbert Park in Ballsbridge;before they went into the park, they stocked up with food at the nearby shop of Johnston, Mooney O' Brien, whose bakery was adjacent. The firm is still trading, even though it's long gone from Ballsbridge. Other early memories included train trips from Harcourt Street station, which was only five minutes' walk from the Quinn house in Upper Camden Street.

When Bernadette became old enough for school proper, she was sent to Warrenmount in the heart of the Liberties. Warrenmount was, and still is, an extraordinary school. The great house that's the heart of the school had once been the home of a certain Nathaniel Warren, who had been a High Sheriff of Dublin in the late 18th century. He named the house 'Warrenmount'.

After his death, the house was sold and on December 1, 1813, the house, together with its estate, became home to a group of Carmelite nuns. During their time at Warrenmount, the Liberties area was suffering from incredible poverty and one of the actions the nuns took to try and help was start a school.

But in 1889, after 76 years at Warrenmount, the Carmelite nuns made a request to the Pope; they wanted to return to a full contemplative life. Their request was granted, on condition that Warrenmount was handed over to Irish nuns. The Presentation Sisters duly took over, with seven of them arriving at Warrenmount on May 6, 1892. They started a national (primary) school there, which is still going strong today. In 2017, the first level school at Warrenmount has 270 pupils, together with such facilities as a whiteboard in every room and full computer facilities, things that would have been unimaginable to the early nuns. Warrenmount also got a secondary school, which is still has.

Until comparatively recently, some of the older nuns at Warrenmount remembered Bernadette's father, Hugh, as a very young boy at the national school, before he "graduated" to the Model School in Inchicore. About 15 years ago, Bernadette took me to meet some of the nuns at Warrenpoint and one or two of the older ones were able to recall her in class.

Bernadette did well at school and she also did all her subjects through Irish, which she has a natural aptitude for; she has often joked that when she was at school, she even did English through Irish! When she was a teenager, she also spent a brief time at a convent school on the northside of Dublin, which she disliked intensely, in preparation for her Leaving Cert. The regime there was so unsympathetic that her father, Hugh, at one stage took time off from work to go and remonstrate with the nuns; Hugh was a most easy going person, so this must have been quite a departure for him.

Bernadette did her Leaving Cert exams at Holy Cross convent on the Crumlin Road and she often told me how she went over there on her bicycle, which she quite happily left outside the convent all day, knowing that it would be perfectly safe. In those days, bicycle thieves in Dublin were a lot rarer than they are today!

When she was 18, she did the entrance exam for the civil service, and was happily surprised when she got the results and found that she had been offered a posting to the Department of External Affairs. Her reaction to this news was that she must have done something right in the exam, especially as some of her friends ended up in much more dreary jobs in such departments as Social Welfare.

Just before starting that job, when Bernadette was about 17, she and a group of friends spent a couple of days cycling in Co Wicklow. They stayed in the old Roundwood Hotel, which is now the Roundwood Inn, oblivious of the fact that the beds were extremely damp. As a result, Bernadette got a bad dose of pleurisy. At that stage, the Quinn family were still living in Upper Camden Street; in the middle of one night, realising how bad Bernadette's condition had got, Bernadette's father knocked up the many doctors who then lived on the South Circular Road, close to its junction with Upper Camden Street. All but one of them pointedly refused to make a call in the middle of the night, regardless of how serious the medical emergency was, but fortunately, one did and saved her life.

But Bernadette took to her new job with alacrity and it soon became obvious that the powers—that—be in charge of the civil service exams had made a good choice. She started at a very junior level but soon found her way round and went on to work in a series of challenging jobs. When she joined, she had to sign the Official Secrets Act and even now, there are many secrets to which she was privy in the Department that she wouldn't dream of revealing to me or anyone else.

She eventually became secretary to the chef de protocol and much of her time was spent organising table plans for state functions, a very intricate task, as people had to be seated so as to avoid any possible diplomatic embarrassment. The first Minister in her 24 years in the Department was Seán McBride, a complex and highly cultured man, whose mother was Maud Gonne.

McBride spent most of his early years in Paris, and the French accent he acquired stayed with him for the rest of his life. But one of her colleagues in her early days in the Department made a poor impression, for good, on Bernadette. A young man from Cork city called Niall Tóibín had started in the Department at about the same time as Bernadette, but he had a penchant for playing practical jokes on his colleagues, which didn't endear him to any of his colleagues, including Bernadette. Fortunately, he left before long and in time, became renowned as one of Ireland's leading actors.

On one occasion, when Bernadette was very junior in the Department, she saw that the Minister' s car had been parked outside the Department offices at Iveagh House for an inordinate length of time, so she told the driver he could motor on. Then a few minutes later the Minister came rushing through, late for an appointment, and was surprised to find no Ministerial car waiting for him. He merely got a taxi instead, wasn't put out at all by the incident and didn't attach any blame to Bernadette.

Iveagh House, St Stephen's Green, Dublin, headquarters of the Department of Foreign Affairs and Trade,where Bernadette spent her entire career. Photo: Hugh Oram

All through Bernadette's career in the Irish foreign service, the family home was at Number 2, Rialto Drive, Dublin. However, she was rarely there, apart from sleeping there at night and on Sundays, as she led a high pressure diplomatic life. In addition to working in the office from 9am until 5pm, Mondays to Fridays, and on Saturday mornings, in the evenings, she often attended diplomatic functions that went on until the small hours of the morning.

Neighbours in Rialto Drive became accustomed to seeing diplomatic cars, their pennants fluttering in the breeze, draw up outside Number 2 to leave Bernadette home after a late function. Photo: Hugh Oram

Three years after she joined the Department, a general election that returned Fianna Fáil to power brought a new Minister to Iveagh House, Frank Aiken. He had been a hardline republican in the north Louth/ south Armagh area during the war of independence and had long been a close associate, perhaps the closest, Éamon de Valera, who first became head of government in 1932. Aiken was the Minister for External Affairs from 1951 until 1954 and then again from 1957 to 1969. He had a reputation for being a gruff and unapproachable man, but Bernadette got on very well with him and on various occasions, when various staff members were away, found herself dealing directly with Frank Aiken in organising State functions. On one occasion, she told me, she was so nervous about working with the top man in the Department that her stomach started rumbling, although he took no notice whatsoever.

From 1954 to 1957, when another Coalition government was in power, the foreign minister was Liam Cosgrave, who in the 1970s, became Taoiseach. Liam Cosgrave, whose father, W. T. Cosgrave, headed the first government after the Irish Free State was set up in 1922, was a very patient and courteous man when he headed the Department of External Affairs. Now in his late 90s, he has retained this courteous affability and his remarkable memory for faces and places. I've talked to him myself and have always found him great company, with a great sense of humour, always withheld from the public! He's also a great man for horse racing. Bernadette remembers that when he was in charge of the department, he took his courtesy to considerable lengths and on the occasions he asked Bernadette to undertake specific work for him, he always went to great trouble to ensure that his request didn't inconvenience her at all.

After the 1957 general election, Frank Aiken returned to the Department. During the early 1960s, the government did much to encourage the process of decolonisation in Africa. Many African delegates came to Dublin and in one famous photograph taken at the time in Iveagh House, the front hall is filled to bursting with African delegates and the only two white faces in the photograph are those of Frank Aiken and Bernadette.

Following on from Aiken was another Fianna Fáil stalwart, Paddy Hillery, by profession a medical doctor. From Co Clare, he always had a mischievous disposition and any time he was in an official car with Bernadette, he was always, with a twinkle in his eye, inviting her to step over the line and have a cuddle or maybe more. But she was always very aware of protocol and decorum and never took up any of his invitations or succumbed to his wandering hands. Later, Hillery became president of Ireland and at one stage, was involved in a huge manufactured scandal as the press began to ask whether he had a mistress lurking in the background.

Shenanigans were always in the mind of some in the department. One well—known character was Con Howard, another Clare man, who had a ferocious reputation for drinking and for chasing women. Bernadette told me that on many occasions, when she was running to sign the attendance book first thing in the morning, Con Howard would sidle up to her and tell her under his breath that he'd love to put his hand between her thighs. Bernadette was skilled at disarming him, telling him "not now Con, I'm running for the book!". Con, despite his diplomatic skills, seen in the way he opened so many doors in Washington to Irish diplomats and politicians, was never appointed an ambassador. Bernadette also often told me the story of another man in the Department, who because he had been active in republican politics in his youth, was always denied promotion, despite his obvious linguistic and other capabilities; eventually, the Department relented and put through a long awaited promotion for him; it came through a week after he had died.

There was always a certain air of divilment behind the austere façade of the Department. On one occasion, Bernadette had arranged to meet a friend who was going to stop his car a little way along Stephen's Green from the Department. One car stopped at the lights and through the open window, Bernadette checked to see if she had the right car and the right driver. It turned out she hadn't and just at that moment, a colleague from the office came along and whispered behind his hand, "so this is how you earn your pin money Bernadette!"

Getting into work on time was often difficult, because of traffic and erratic bus schedules, especially after the family had moved to Rialto. There were other distractions, too, such as Bang Bang, a well—known Dublin character of the time. In those days, when the entrance to buses was open and people could jump on and off at will, Bang Bang used to do just that. Bernadette was always keen to ensure that her hair looked just perfect, for all the diplomatic functions she had to attend. She became very friendly with two young hairdressers, Peter and Mark Kavanagh, who had just started their first salon, in Grafton Street; today, Peter Mark is the largest hairdressing chain in Ireland. But on one infamous occasion, when Bernadette had just had her hair done, she was holding the rail, preparing to get off a bus, when Bang Bang crept up behind her and started stroking her hair. She was rightly furious, but could do nothing, otherwise she risked falling off the bus.

Other 'stars' in the Department may have been just as controversial, but for entirely different reasons. Dr Conor Cruise O'Brien long worked in the Department, where his future second wife, poet Máire Mhac an tSaoi, daughter of Sean McEntee, a former government minister, also worked. On one memorable occasion, after Bernadette and I had become an item, Conor and Máire invited us to drinks in a well—known gay bar, Bartley Dunnes, in Dublin city centre, long since demolished. The end result of that particular meeting was some very stimulating and controversial conversation.

Bernadette's final minister was Dr Garret FitzGerald, known for his probity and also famed for asking whether if some particular idea worked well in theory, it would work well in practice. He often had an absent minded air about him, on occasion, seen electioneering wearing two odd socks.

She was very friendly with the top people in all three parties, Fianna Fáil, Fine Gael and Labour and managed to preserve her neutrality. One party leader with whom she was particularly friendly was Brendan Corish, a leader of the Labour Party, who had become leader of the Labour Party on 1960, and they would often joke about all the trouble he'd have to go to arranging a baby sitter at home in Wexford, so that he could come to a State function in Dublin. She was also very friendly with Charlie Haughey, who later became Ireland's most controversial as well as most corrupt Taoiseach. When Charlie Haughey was a minister, he was often involved in State functions and always made a point of staying behind afterwards to make sure that the catering staff were well looked after. Charlie Haughey had lots of time for Bernadette and always referred to her as "her little pet".

Another Fianna Fáil politician with whom she got on well with was Éamon de Valera, Taoiseach until 1959 and then president of Ireland for 14 years. By the time he became president, his eyesight was in serious deterioration, and Bernadette was tasked to undertake a very delicate mission every time a big State function was held. It became her job to guide de Valera around, because his eyesight was so bad, and make sure that he didn't bump into anyone or worse still, fall over. Her fluent Irish was a big help, as de Valera was always keen to speak Irish whenever he could. Bernadette also became friendly with Dev's delightful wife, Sinéad.

One or two politicians were far from friendly. One such was Mícheál Ó Móráin (1912—1983), who was a solicitor from Castlebar, Co Mayo. He was a long time member of Fianna Fáil and held various ministerial portfolios. The longest of these was as Minister for Lands, a job he held between 1959 and 1968. But Ó Móráin had an unquenchable thirst and at various functions, he was often in a very drunken state. He had had various run—ins with a senior official in the Department of External Affairs, to whom Bernadette was very close, and any time he bumped into Bernadette at a function, a seriously drunken Ó Móráin accosted her in the rudest fashion imaginable. There was nothing she could do about him, except take no notice, in other words, be extremely diplomatic.

But other occasions were much more memorable, for all the right reasons. In 1961, Prince Rainier from Monaco and his wife, the former American film actress, Grace Kelly, came to Ireland for the first royal visit since 1922. A State reception was held in the Gresham Hotel, for which Bernadette practised her French and also her curtseys, so she was able to perform them both to perfection when she met the royal couple. At one stage, someone else she met who was very much in the news was Group Captain Peter Townsend, who then seemed likely to marry Princess Margaret, the Queen's sister, although it never happened.

Her most memorable meeting was when the then US president, John F.

At the Gresham Hotel,Dublin,in 1961,during the visit to Ireland by Prince Rainier and Princess Grace of Monaco,Bernadette met the royal couple and chatted with them in French. It was the first royal visit to Ireland since the Irish Free State had been set up in 1922. Photo: Hugh Oram

Kennedy, came to Ireland at the end of June, 1963. One night, a State banquet was held in Iveagh House. Bernadette was introduced to Kennedy, who was immediately smitten with her. He led her up the big staircase in Iveagh House by her little finger, and soon made her an offer. He wanted her to come to Washington and settle in there but knowing Kennedy's avidity for sexual relations, it became a family joke at home that he really wanted to take her to Washington with just one thing in mind. Bernadette's boss at the time, Gerry Woods, was well tanked up and got wind of what was going on. He stormed over to Kennedy and said: "Mister President, you're not having her, she's mine", not the usual way in which a US President is addressed!

Some weeks later, Bernadette was at a diplomatic party in Dublin, all dressed up in a very white dress with full length sleeves. At that stage in her life, she had her very own dressmaker, Miss Bone, who lived in Rehobath Place, just off the South Circular Road, and close to the Quinn family home in Rialto. At this particular party, a diplomat managed to spill a glass of red wine down one of the sleeves of Bernadette's dress and she saw it as an ominous omen. Tragically it was, as not long after, on November 22, 1963, Kennedy was killed by assassin's bullets at Dallas in Texas.

During the visit to Ireland in 1963 by then US President, John F. Kennedy, he visited Árás an Uachtaráin, the official residence in Dublin of the President of Ireland.

The photograph shows from left, Seán Lemass, Taoiseach; his wife, Kathleen; Sinéad de Valera, wife of the then President of Ireland; President John F. Kennedy; Eunice Kennedy Shriver, Kennedy's sister and President Éamon de Valera.

Bernadette worked closely on the visit and was in the Árás during Kennedy's visit there. After the assassination of Kennedy in Dallas on November 22, 1963, she received a letter of commendation from the US Embassy in Dublin for all the work she had done on the Kennedy visit to Ireland earlier that year.
Photo: Irish Press

The old Rialto cinema in Dublin

Before Kennedy came to Ireland, the US ambassador to Ireland was a very colourful character called Scott McLeod. He had the US ambassador to Ireland from 1957 until 1961 and Bernadette became exceptionally friendly with him. Earlier on, in the earlier 1950s, he had been very involved in the McCarthy campaign. He had also had a career in the FBI before becoming head of State Department security. He had come to Ireland with a very controversial image, but while here, was a popular ambassador. Bernadette's friendship with him was a sure sign of how she was able to handle the most difficult public figures with consummate diplomacy.

Scott McLeod served as US ambassador to Ireland until February, 1961. When he was leaving, he wrote Bernadette a very touching and gentle letter. She had enjoyed a great friendship with him and when the news came through in November that same year, 1961, that he had died from a heart attack, aged 47, it was a genuinely shocking experience for her. His successor in Dublin was Edward Stockdale, with whom she was also on friendly terms, but not as intimate as her friendship with Scott McLeod, who was survived by his wife Edna and their three children and when the new US Embassy in Ballsbridge was officially opened on May 23, 1964, to replace the one at 15 Merrion Square, the ceremony was performed by Scott McLeod's widow, Edna.

In 1970, another US president visited Ireland, Richard Nixon. If Kennedy's visit in 1963 was full of charisma and charm, Nixon's was the exact opposite. Nixon came here in 1970 partly to trace his Quaker roots. His physical appearance was in dull contrast to that of Kennedy; the blue shadow on Nixon's face, that he couldn't eradicate by shaving, was as offputting as his dull and dreary manner.

Bernadette remembered vividly being at a State function in Dublin Castle; there, she got into conversation with the then taoiseach, Jack Lynch, who was as bored as everyone else with the tedium of the Nixon visit. At the time, Lynch was also surrounded by the controversy of the arms trial and Lynch joked in a macabre way, to Bernadette, that it was a pity that someone didn't shoot him!

During her time in the Department, Bernadette had several jobs. For a number of years, she worked as secretary to the chef de protocol and was heavily involved in organising State functions. She remembers in particular, when Maírtín Ó Flaitheartaigh (Martin O' Flaherty) was the secretary to President de Valera.

Bernadette in Paris. Photo: Hugh Oram

Maírtín always insisted on speaking Irish and he'd often phone Bernadette at home first thing in the morning to discuss a State dinner that was being organised that night. He and she had to go through all the table plans, in Irish, to make sure that everyone would be sitting in their proper place.

She also had a long stint in film making. In the late 1950s and into the 1960s, the Department commissioned many films, for cultural and tourism reasons. Bernadette got to know many of the leading film makers of the time, such as Paddy Carey and George Fleischmann. The latter was a particularly interesting character. He had trained in film making in his native Germany before the second world war, then became a pilot in the Luftwaffe. His plane came down in Ireland in 1941 and he spent the rest of the war in very easy—going internment at the Curragh in Co Kildare. The Irish government soon discovered his film making skills and they were put to good use for the State. He spent most of his subsequent career in Ireland, but moved to Canada for the last few years of his life; he died there in a ridiculous accident when he was out roller skating.

Other film makers with she had a long professional relationship included Louis Marcus, one of the stars of Irish filming making, and a film producer from London called George Grafton—Greene and his wife, Brigid. Film makers often have spectacular temperaments and when the civil service bureaucracy, never a good mix with the creative skills needed for film making, produced inevitable delays, it was always Bernadette who managed to placate the film directors.

One person with whom Bernadette had close professional liaisons was a would—be film maker called Tom Kennedy, who had sent several film script developments into the Department. Bernadette became close friends with Tom and his Dutch wife, Appie, who had got married at the same time as ourselves. Later, when I published the first book under my own name, the book about Bewley's, which came out at the end of 1980, Tom was the publisher.

Bernadette always had great skills as a trouble shooter and at one stage in her career, when she was walking along St Stephen's Green to the office, Hector Fabron, the head chef at the nearby Russell Hotel, would often be lying in wait for her. The Russell Hotel, which closed down just over 40 years ago, did much catering for the Department. But Hector always had a plaintive plea: "When is the Department going to pay me?". Bernadette always managed to be very diplomatic and assuage the irate feelings of Hector Fabron.

Bernadette was good friends with many other well—known people. She was particularly friendly with Major Vivion de Valera, a son of Éamon de Valera. His father had founded the Irish Press newspaper in 1931, so it was inevitable that Vivion would one day take over as managing director. During his time at the Irish Press, he was seen by the staff as a benevolent despot, even though he was both kindly and eccentric. He never forgot when he first arrived at the Irish Press; he set out to meet all the staff and found the sub—editors missing en masse. Instead of being hard at work, they were all frolicking in a nearby pub. After Vivion's time at the Irish Press, the newspaper group got enmeshed in a sea of troubles, which weren't helped by a weak and inept management. The group closed in 1995.

Another person in the media with whom Bernadette was very friendly was P. P. O' Reilly from RTÉ. P. P. was born and brought up in Liverpool; his parents were Irish emigrants there. He returned to Ireland and served in the defence forces during the second world war 'emergency'. After the war, he started a long career in broadcasting by joining Radio Éireann; after the Irish television service started in 1962, he soon made a name for himself producing and presenting programmes such as Broadsheet. When the troubles erupted in the North in 1969, he was RTÉ's Belfast correspondent. When Dana from Derry won Eurovision in 1970, he was on the plane bringing her back to Ireland; later, P. P. told us the real story of the young singer's life in Derry. Then in the 1970s, P. P. moved back to radio and for years, he did the newspaper review slot after the 8am news; he was renowned for being a stickler for correct pronunciation. Bernadette often met him when he was hosting lavish international gatherings for RTÉ in such places as the old Royal Hibernian Hotel in Dawson Street. One of their favourite meeting places was Rice's pub, at the corner of St Stephen's Green and South King Street, a pub that was later demolished to make way for the Stephen's Green shopping centre.

Rice's pub, on the corner of St Stephen's Green and South King Street, Dublin. Here, Bernadette often went for drinks with a good friend from RTÉ, P.P.O'Reilly. The pub was demolished in the late 1980s to make way for the St Stephen's Green shopping centre

I too became great friends with P. P. In his personal life, he had troubling times with his wife Antoinette, who was an alcoholic. For years, they lived on the Dublin Road in Bray, but later, moved to Naas, Co Kildare, where Antoinette's family ran a pub on the Main Street. The last time that I met P. P. was at that pub, not long before he died in 1995; his health had deteriorated so badly that he couldn't stop wheezing.

Someone else whom Bernadette knew well was John O'Donovan, a remarkable literary figure, an expert on George Bernard Shaw, as well as on music. Later on, he became equalled renowned on RTÉ radio as a presenter for many years of the "Dear Sir or Madame" programme of listeners' letters. He also had a great liking for walking in the Dublin Mountains and in her younger days, Bernadette often found herself accompanying him on his walking expeditions, being bombarded with innumerable examples of his literary and musical knowledge. Bernadette was also a keen concert goer, to concerts given by the national radio station's symphony orchestra. She'd often find herself sandwiched between John O'Donovan, there to do a review for the Evening Press newspaper, and Charles Acton, doing the same for The Irish Times. Both men were highly impressed by the ease with which Bernadette could read a musical score, a trait inherited from her father.

The last time that she saw John O'Donovan was in 1970. After Bernadette and I had met for the first time, in the Department, we had our first date and she waited for me outside the GPO. Who should walk past but John O'Donovan. He died in 1985, aged 64.

Another person she knew well was Todd Andrews, grandfather of RTÉ personality Ryan Tubridy. Todd Andrews, a Fianna Fáil stalwart, had had a varied career, including at the head of Bord na Mona, the State—owned peat processing company, and of CIE, the State—owned transport company. At one stage, when Andrews was chairman of the RTÉ Authority, he had an embarrassing (for him) encounter with Bernadette, who had been responsible for sending out all the invitations to a high profile State dinner. Andrews complained bitterly and inaccurately that he had never received his invitation and his complaint went as far as a question in the Dáil. It was very upsetting for Bernadette, who was always meticulous in every aspect of her work.

Then Todd Andrews found that the invitation had been delivered to his home in Dundrum, but had somehow got lost. He was fulsome in his apologies to Bernadette and told her than in his capacity as chairman of the RTÉ Authority, he would ensure that its radio side would bring in a poetry programme and put her in charge of presenting it. But Bernadette graciously declined the offer, even though it would have given her poetry career a headstart.

Her many personal friends included Myra Maguire, whom Bernadette often met during her lunch break, which she usually took in Grafton Street, going to places like Brown Thomas for lunch. Myra had been brought up in Scotland, but came to live in Ireland at an early age, when her father was made a manager for the Ford motor company here. The family lived for many years in Leinster Road, Rathmines. Myra was a remarkably talented artist and Bernadette got to know her because Myra did the letters of credence for ambassadors new to Dublin. Sometimes, there were mistakes in the scripts given to Myra, and when the ambassadors asked her to redo the letters, her response was always that she' d be happy to redraw them, provided she was paid accordingly. Myra ended up as a professor at the National College of Art & Design. After she died in 2015, I attended her funeral in the Presbyterian church in Harcourt Road; at that stage, Bernadette was unable to leave the house, so she was unable to attend.

Another personal friend, from Bernadette's earlier days, was a kindly, white haired lady called Kitty Walsh, who had once worked in the Bailey Son & Gibson paper bag making factory at Dolphin' s Barn. Kitty and her cousin Kathleen Walsh were long standing friends of Bernadette' s mother. Many tales were told about Kathleen, like the time when she had gone to the pictures, but had to stand up in the middle of the performance because her legs had got the cramps. Anguished shouts went out: "Sit down, sit down!". On another occasion, when Kathleen was swimming in Dublin Bay, she came face to face with a floating turd, which made for some hilarious subsequent conversations. Years after Kathleen had died, Bernadette and I continued to go and visit Kitty regularly at her flat just behind Whitefriars Street church. She was the most loving and generous of people and it was always a pleasure to have a chat with her.

In Bernadette' s later life, after we had got married, we got very friendly with Theodora Fitzgibbon, probably the best restaurant critic The Irish Times ever had, and her husband George Morrison, the documentary film maker responsible for such productions as Mise Éire and An Tine Bheo. On one memorable occasion in the Isle of

Man, we met up with them. Four of us were crammed into a tiny Mini car and at one stage, Theodora announced at the top of her voice: "If you don' t stop this car immediately, I shall wee wee in the seat".

Life with the two of them, especially Theodora, was never dull!

One of the many very talented people in the Department whom Bernadette got to know well was Tommy Woods, who managed to have a double career, as he wrote a weekly column for The Irish Times under the nom de plume of Thucycides. He was sent to Strasbourg to represent Ireland on the Council of Europe. He wasn' t the first or indeed the last Irish person to be sent on appointment to Strasbourg who managed to drink themselves to death there. Tommy died in the aptly named Hotel Terminus in the centre of Strasbourg. Ironically, when we made our last foreign trip together, in 1991, it was to Strasbourg and we were staying in an hotel that was almost next door to the Hotel Terminus.

Bernadette had begun her poetry career in 1951, when she first had a poem published, in Ireland' s Own. She carried on writing poetry for 35 years, with some of her poetry continuing to be published up until the mid-1980s. One of the last media outlets in which she published was, fittingly, The Irish Times. She wrote her poetry in both English and Irish and during her Gaelic League days, when she became very friendly with someone from Brittany, and his family, she often wrote and published in French. Much of her poetry was published by the long defunct Cork Weekly Examiner, which paid a handsome 10/—per poem.

Bernadette pictured outside the Irish Embassy in Paris, during one of our many trips to France.
Photo: Hugh Oram

She always gave her address as 80 St Stephen' s Green, Dublin, which of course was the headquarters of the Department of External Affairs. But that had one drawback; a Scot in exile discovered her poetry and pursued Bernadette by letter for some considerable time. The 'tartan terror' or the thistle blower,nom de plume ' Driftwood', just wouldn' t be put off and Bernadette had considerable trouble in persuading him to stop writing to her. On the 'plus' side, when the Guinness company in Dublin sponsored an annual poetry competition in the late 1950s, it was very prestigious and attracted many of the best—known poets of the day; Bernadette was nominated for it on three occasions, quite an accolade in itself.

Most of Bernadette' s poetry was written in the 1950s. In the 1960s, her diplomatic life was too hectic to permit much spare time for writing poetry, but in the 1960s, she was being published in two prestigious magazines, Creation and Irishwoman' s Journal.

Bernadette had met Sean O' Sullivan, a very talented Irish—American journalist, who around 1960, was features editor of Creation magazine, founded in the late 1950s. Sean then looked like being made features editor of The Irish Times, but the management there dithered so much that it never happened. In the meantime, Sean got a job offer for something else he had applied for, in the Netherlands, and he felt obliged to take that post. When he eventually returned home to Dublin, he founded Irishwoman' s Journal and Bernadette began writing for that.

Much later, when we were settled in Dublin, Bernadette again began publishing, in such magazines as Social & Personal. In 1983, she also published in The Irish Times, which turned out to the swansong for her poetic career. In those days, The Irish Times paid the grand sum of £20 for a poem and recently I found one of her payslips from The Irish Times.

Such was Bernadette's schedule at work that she hardly ever seemed to be at home. From Mondays to Fridays, as well as on Saturday mornings, she had a full timetable of work. Then inevitably, in the evenings, there' d be a function to attend, either hosted by the government or by one of the many embassies in Dublin. Those embassies all knew Bernadette well and when a new ambassador arrived in Ireland, he or sometimes she, was always given Bernadette' s name as their first port of call, the person who could sort out anything that needed sorting out. She had given an early example of being a stickler for getting things done properly and accurately. On her 21st birthday, when the family was still living at Upper Camden Street, she was given a big birthday celebration. But a newspaper reporter turned up, complete with photographer, but the subsequent report was so full of inaccuracies that Bernadette was upset for days afterwards and even retold the tale to me on various occasions after we had got married.

Sometimes, parties at embassies were full of high jinks, such as one occasion, when Bernadette found herself wrapped up inside a carpet together with an ambassador. It was, she later assured people, all innocent fun! But her nightly ritual of functions meant that often, she didn' t get home until four in the morning; she was still required to be back at work at nine o' clock. So home often meant a cup of coffee, a quick snooze and that was that, except for the weekends. On more than one occasion, a 'do' at the Department went on so long that Bernadette ended up sleeping in the apartment at Iveagh House occupied by the person in charge of cleaning.

Being away from home so much meant that she had too little time for the family cats. Bernadette has always been a devoted cat lover and her mother looked after a constant procession of cats at home in Rialto Drive. But Bernadette did take her holiday allowances and did her stint of trips abroad. Her first trip outside the country was when she was 17 and went on a trip to Wales with the Gaelic League. In 1951, when she was 21, she and a couple of friends went on a holiday to the Tirol in Austria. It was Bernadette's first visit to Paris, which made a big impression on her, followed by a long train trip to Austria. She and her friends stayed in a small mountain village called Igls, near Innsbruck in western Austria. Over 30 years later, when Bernadette and I visited Igls, we met up with the man who was managing the pension where Bernadette and her friends stayed in 1951, Herr Gruber, and we were delighted to find that he had clear memories of that 1951 visit to the village.

Bernadette also told me how that 1951 trip had nearly never happened. The tickets for the onward journey from Paris were being organised by Thomas Cook, the travel agents. Bernadette found that Cook' s Paris office hadn' t got everything ready; while she pacing up and down the platform at the Gare de l' Est in Paris, with the train to Innsbruck about to depart, a man from Thomas Cook came running along the platform, shouting "Mademoiselle Quinn". She caught the train to Austria, just!

In the 1960s, Bernadette went to France on a few occasions with her sister Gloria and her fiancé, Eamonn Williams. On several occasions, they stayed in a family—run hotel in Paris and kept in touch with that family, the Riegels, for many years afterwards. During one of their trips to the south of France, the three of them stayed in a remarkable hotel at Mougins in Provence, which turned out to be owned by Prince Sihanouk of Cambodia (1922—2012). He was king of Cambodia from 1941 until 1955 and then from 1993 to 2004; he also managed to produce 50 films and wrote a similar number of musical compositions. At home in Ireland after we had got married, we often went with Gloria and Eamonn for Sunday afternoon excursions to Co Kildare.

Also at home, Bernadette was ahead of her time in another way. For a time as a young girl, she was very religious and used to go to church regularly. But as she grew older, she lost all interest in religion and in her 20s, decided that she was no longer going to go to Mass on Sundays. In the 1950s, that was practically unheard of and what was even more amazing was the fact that her parents, Hugh and Mary or May, never once chastised for for skipping Mass. Since then, I have rarely if ever heard Bernadette express any interest in any organised religion.

In the mid—1960s, a family tragedy struck. Kevin was the brother of Eamonn Wiliams, who later married Bernadette' s sister Gloria; Kevin tried a great many careers but never stuck with any of them. But he had a great interest in the sea and about 1964, he went to a boat show in the RDS and promptly bought a boat. He was so keen to try it out that he immediately took it to Skerries, a seaside town with which his family had long connections. He and his friends ignored the very strong warnings from local fishermen that they shouldn' t put to sea, because a big storm was brewing. Their advice was ignored and a short time later, in the midst of a ferocious storm, the boat capsized and all on board were lost; their bodies were never recovered. The following morning, at 8 o' clock, Bernadette turned on the 8am radio news to hear about the disappearance of Kevin and his companions.

Long before I came on the scene, Bernadette had a long personal relationship with someone senior to her in the Department of External Affairs, who later became Irish Ambassador to Argentina. Michael Leo Skentleberry was born in November, 1917; his father was A. H. Skentlebury, who lived at Crosshaven, Co Cork. His son, Leo, was educated at the famous 'North Mon' in Cork city before going on to join the Department. In the earlier 1950s, he was chargé d' affaires in the Irish embassy at Canberra in Australia. One of the sights he saw there and indeed filmed, was Ronnie Delany winning a gold medal for Ireland at the Melbourne Olympics in 1954. After Leo returned from Australia in 1957, he worked in Iveagh House, Dublin, becoming chef de protocol. Then on April 16, 1964, he presented his credentials to the President of Argentina and and settled in to become Irish ambassador in Buenos Aires.

But while he was stationed in Buenos Aires, he developed Parkinson' s Disease, which became more and more severe, so much so that he had to return to Ireland and retire from the foreign service. Bernadette and Leo had been close for a long time and they had planned to marry; Bernadette relished the thought of being the Ambassador' s wife; she would have dealt with all the diplomatic parties with great dexterity. It was not to be; when Leo realised that he was developing a progressive and incurable illness, he decided it would be unfair for him to marry Bernadette and impose the task of looking after him on her. So much to her regret, the marriage plans were called off, a bitter blow for her. Leo had long before been introduced to Bernadette' s family. Her father, Hugh, was concerned beforehand that Leo might have been a high falutin' diplomat, difficult to get on with, but he turned out to be the exact opposite, a warm and gentle person.

After he retired, Leo went to live in the Standard Hotel in Harcourt Street in Dublin; he eventually married his housekeeper. He died on March 11, 1990, at the age of 72. Ironically, he had been 13 years older than Bernadette, while I am 13 years younger. Leo' s funeral Mass was held at St Mary' s in Haddington Road, Dublin. Bernadette attended and met many of her former diplomatic colleagues, including Noel Dorr, who for many years held the highest ranking civil service posts in the Department, yet is a most down—to—earth person. Noel attended Leo' s funeral and Bernadette noted that Noel had gone to the church straight from the office, carrying not one, but two jam—packed briefcases, one in each hand. The occasion was also Bernadette' s way of saying farewell to the foreign service as she never attended any functions with diplomats after that.

In a previous relationship, long before Leo, Bernadette came to know a journalist who worked for what was then the Cork Examiner, based in its Dublin office, then in Grafton Street. Throughout the 1950s, Bernadette was publishing some of her poetry in the old Cork Weekly Examiner, and met up with the journalist in the Examiner' s Dublin office. He eventually gave up journalism and opted for an academic life in Perth, western Australia, where he became a professor. At one stage, it seemed likely that the two of them would marry, but after the journalist concerned promptly announced that he was emigrating to Australia; Bernadette pointedly refused to follow suit.

From 1990 onwards, the only former diplomatic colleague she sometimes met was Robert McDonagh, who had a high flying career in the Department, from which he retired in 1989. Robert' s wife had tragically died just as Robert was retiring, so Robert, or Bob as everyone knew him, lived on his own in a flat at the corner of Wellington Road and Clyde Road, Ballsbridge. His two sons, Robert and Philip, also went into the foreign service, where they too have had high flying careers. Bob, the father, died in 2015. Bob had a very puckish sense of humour; he was in charge of the retiring party for Bernadette at the Department in June, 1972, just before we got married. He had announced, in his very droll style, that the enormous dining room table in the staff canteen was going to be Bernadette' s present from the Department. For one split second, everyone, including Bernadette, thought that Bob was being serious!

Bernadette stayed in the Department, which by then had changed its name to the Department of Foreign Affairs (in recent years, the much more prosaic words 'and Trade' have been added to its title), until 1972, when we got married. I had first met Bernadette I the summer of 1970, when she was working in the Department's press office. When we got married, the ridiculously antiquated rule that female civil servants had to leave their jobs on marriage, still applied. It was repealed the following year, 1973, but we had moved on at that stage and Bernadette never returned to her old job.

Bernadette's marriage

The summer of 1970 turned out to be a fateful one for us. I was living and working in Belfast, earning a precarious living as a freelance journalist, interspersed with periods on the dole. In August, 1970, I was working on a feature for a Belfast daily newspaper on the mining industry in Ireland. At that time, exciting things were in the pipeline for the mining industry, both north and south. On Thursday, August 13, 1970, there was a cheap day excursion to Dublin, so I decided to go to Dublin and go round the relevant Government departments to glean further information for my article.

The last call of the day was to the Department of Foreign Affairs, where I thought I might source some additional useful information. The woman in the press office who should have taken my call was on the phone, so she asked Bernadette to go downstairs and look after the journalist in the entrance hall in Iveagh House. Bernadette was her usual helpful self, which was useful for the article I was putting together, but much more importantly, there was an instant spark between us. People often talk of love at first sight and it's perfectly true, it does happen, and it happened in our case. Within a week, we were doing a line and we soon discovered that we had so much in common. I joked afterwards that it must have been my 'kipper' tie that had attracted her!

Yet the first time that I met Bernadette after then would have been very inauspicious if it hadn't been for Bernadette. We had arranged to meet outside the GPO one day at 1pm. I was so short of cash that I hitched hiked down from Belfast, but the lifts were very slow in coming, so that by the time I got to the GPO, I was an hour late. Thankfully, Bernadette was patient and waited for me; I was so relieved to see her again. A short while later, we went on our first protracted date, coffee in a small café, long since gone, at the corner of Upper Merrion Street and Lower Baggot Street. Then we strolled down to Pearse railway station in Westland Row and took the train out to Greystones.

Despite the fact that Bernadette was living and working in Dublin and I was doing the same in Belfast, we managed to keep in regular contact. On another occasion, we had a great time on Bull Island at Dollymount on the northside of Dublin. I decided to hitch back to Belfast that night, but couldn't get any further than Dundalk. I knew I'd have to find somewhere for the night, so a kindly Garda in the Garda barracks there directed to a very run—down hostel than had once been the workhouse. None of this deterred us in any way and soon came the next step, going home to meet Bernadette's parents.

I had had a miserable time living in England, including a frightful time at school, until I eventually quit England to come and live in Ireland, going to university in that most Irish of cities, Derry. I had made my first trip to Ireland when I came to Dublin, by myself, when I was just 14. I found myself instinctively drawn towards

Ireland and its people, but curiously, it wasn't until many years later that all the Irish connections in my family were uncovered. It was only two years ago that I discovered my earliest relative in Ireland, a woman called Mary Whelan, born in Waterford city in 1790.

If I had any trepidation about meeting Bernadette's parents, it was immediately dispelled. They couldn't have been more loving and generous as well as being great fun and they turned out to be almost surrogate parents for me. I quickly grew very fond of them and always enjoyed going to their house in Rialto, Dublin. Sunday lunches were always times of great joy and fun. When I first met Bernadette, her father was just two years retired from his work on the railways and I was very fortunate to have enjoyed his company for a further 18 years, until he died in 1988. I got on similarly well with Bernadette's mother May, who survived her husband by nine years and died in 1997. It's a small mark of the respect and affection in which I hold them that on their respective anniversaries, I always go to visit their grave at St Fintan's in Sutton on the northside of Dublin, close to Howth Head.

I also got on well with Bernadette's sister Gloria and her husband Eamonn, who had got married a couple of years before Bernadette and I got married.

Almost as soon as we'd started our relationship, we began our extensive travels the length and breadth of Europe, especially in France. During one memorable 10 day period, we flew three times between Dublin and Paris, which we had to do because of my work commitments in Dublin.

The photo was taken in the railway museum at Mulhouse in eastern France and shows a poster depicting the vintage era of French rail travel. The Cité du Train is a fascinating place, the largest railway museum in Europe and one of the 10 largest in the world. Many of our travels through France over the years were done by train. Photo: Hugh Oram

SUMMER ON THE FRENCH RIVIERA BY THE BLUE TRAIN

For nearly two years, from 1970 to 1972, despite the fact that there was a full scale war going on in the North, Bernadette and I met up every weekend. She got off early from work on Friday afternoons to take the train to Belfast, where she'd spend the weekend with me. We went to all kinds of delightful places in the North, from Portaferry, Donaghadee and Bangor in Co Down to Ballycastle I north Antrim. I always remember that on Sunday evenings, I'd take Bernadette back to the railway station for her train home to Dublin. Outside the old railway station in Great Victoria Street, a Salvation Army band played, every Sunday night, and their music has formed an indelible memory.

Before too long, Bernadette and I started talking about getting married. Neither of us wanted a big church wedding in Dublin, followed by a party that would be attended by family, friends and hundreds of hangers—on, people to whom we would never give even the time of day! Instead, we cast about to find somewhere outside Ireland where we could be easily married. Long before the Internet, we soon found that we could literally turn up in the Isle of Man and get married the following day, which is precisely what we did. We settled on the small fishing town of Peel on the west coast of the island, made contact on a Monday with the diocesan office in Douglas and the Trinity College, Dublin, educated vicar in Peel, Rev McCullough. All the documentation was sorted on the Monday and on the Tuesday, June 27, 1972, we got married at St German's Anglican church in Peel—it's now a cathedral—with my sister Kate, who had flown in from London, as the bridesmaid. The church warden, Bob Shimmin, was the other witness. Bernadette's parents were very understanding about our decision; they didn't travel over to the Isle of Man but on two subsequent occasions, we took them on holiday there.

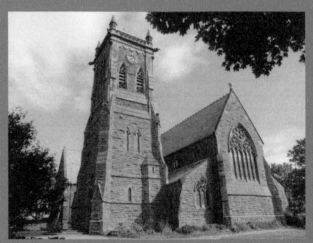

St German's, Peel, Isle of Man, where Bernadette and Hugh were married on June 27,1972.
Photo: North American Manx Association

We had found a lovely place to stay in Peel, a b and b on Victoria Terrace, run by the Davies, a lovely couple from Lancashire who had long lived on the island, where Arthur worked as a postman. We became firm friends with Arthur and his wife, Ruth, until the end of their lives. On the afternoon of the wedding, they organised a sherry party in their front room, just them and us and my sister.

We formed a great affection for the Isle of Man and the way we were treated there with such warmth and generosity. We went back several times to stay in Peel and on two occasions, Bernadette's parents were delighted to be back on the island. They had honeymooned on the island in 1928.

Then it was back to sordid reality, after the wedding. Our return to Dublin by ship from the Isle of Man was fraught with difficulties, as the ship managed to get stuck on a sandbank coming into Dublin port. Then it was a return to Belfast. We left the small flat I had and moved into a much more spacious apartment in a leafy and pleasant area of east Belfast. The only trouble we had turned out to be with the landlady, who owned the house and lived downstairs. She was related to the great Irish poet, W. B. Yeats, so I can only say, charitably, that she must have come from the illiberal and reactionary branch of the family. She kept pestering Bernadette to change her name, because it sounded too Irish and too Catholic, which we thought was a ridiculous request, but perhaps understandable given the paranoia created by sectarian conflicts in the North. But in general, we found everyone in the North, regardless of their religious and political persuasions, welcoming.

One of my best friends work wise was Brum Henderson, then the managing director of Ulster Television, who sometimes invited me to splendid and over—the—top lunches at the television station. On another occasion, I couldn't go on a press trip to London so Bernadette went instead of me. Judging by what she told me afterwards, she was the only person who didn' t spend that night bed hopping and that included some of the well—known female onscreen faces from UTV! On other occasions, Bernadette was pursued by a senior journalist from that staunchly Unionist newspaper, the Newsletter, who had taken a great shine to her while someone else who became very enamoured of her was a reporter from the Daily Express newspaper in London. By now a respectably married lady, she dealt with all her admirers in the Belfast media with the same aplomb she' d shown towards the mad Scottish admirer of her poetry in earlier years!

We stayed in Belfast for two years;I was building up my journalistic career and one of the people I was working for published a lot of magazines aimed at the wedding and home improvement markets. It was easy enough to run off a few thousand words on any given topic and Bernadette joined in, putting her writing skills to work. But in 1974, the North descended into much more chaos than usual when loyalist strikes brought the place to a virtual halt. We decided that enough was enough, packed all our possessions into a Mini car and drove south, getting through before all the roads were closed. We eventually got to Dundalk where I must admit I was very relieved to see a Garda on duty, to whom we explained what we were doing.

Despite no longer living in Belfast, I was spending a couple of days a week in Belfast, editing various magazines, an awful chore, while spending another two days week doing likewise in Dublin. The sensible thing was to live somewhere halfway between the two cities, so we plumped on Drogheda, where we spent three very enjoyable years. The first year was spent in a delapidated cottage at Colpe, on the southern outskirts of Drogheda; then Colpe was mostly made up of farms, but now the whole area is covered with vast housing estates. We were lucky because our landlord was a really decent guy, Tony Mathews, who was a journalist working for the Evening Press and RTÉ in Dublin, and whose sister Anne was for years a journalist on the Drogheda Independent. Then with the help of a £12 per month fixed rate mortgage from the old Drogheda Corporation, we bought a new semi—detached house on the Oaklawn estate, off the North Road in Drogheda.

Bernadette soon turned herself into a determined homemaker and soon had the place very comfortable. We also made many friends in Drogheda, such as John Callan, who was then running a delightful craft shop and café in Narrow West Street. Bernadette was the one who encouraged John to get married, which he did, to Jane, a nurse in Drogheda. The town was a pleasant place and in the 1970s, West Street, the main throughfare, was a bustling place full of shops. But much and all as we enjoyed living in Drogheda, the strain of doing all the commuting was getting to me, so in 1977, we sold the house and moved to Dublin.

Despite everything, we managed to do plenty of foreign trips, starting off with Paris, which did before we were married, then taking in such cities as Amsterdam and Berlin and countries from Greece to Portugal, and one of our most memorable trips of all, a fortnight long bus trip round the whole of Poland when it was still a communist country.

Our new home in Dublin was a flat on the Clonskeagh Road in south Dublin. The early years there were pleasant, although in later years, neighbour troubles made it much less pleasant. While we were away on a trip to mainland Europe, the flat was broken into, very much an inside job by someone living very close by. We arrived home from Dublin airport one night to find the front door of the flat broken open and the place inside in a state of chaos. Bernadette was particularly upset because the low life burglars had stolen the memento of the 1963 Kennedy visit to Ireland given to Bernadette by the US Embassy in Dublin as a token of appreciation for all her work on the visit. But we gradually got ourselves together after that unpleasant shock.

Bernadette pictured outside St German's church, now cathedral, in Peel, Isle of Man, in 1978. We'd taken Bernadette's parents, Hugh and May for a holiday there.

Hugh Quinn, examining an Isle of Man steam train, 1978.

Hugh and May Quinn with Bernadette on a
horse tram in Douglas, Isle of Man, 1978.

This was long one of our favourite brasseries in
our favourite arrondissement in Paris, the 7th. Le
Saint-Germain is on one of the busiest crossroads
in this part of Paris, so it was always great fun to
sit on the terrace and watch the world saunter
past, on foot, or drive past in the usual alarming
Parisian driving style.
Menu cover: Le Saint-Germain, Paris

Bernadette and Hugh outside St
German's church, Peel, in 1978

Hugh and May Quinn, Bernadette's parents, on a
horse tram in Douglas, Isle of Man.
All photos by Hugh Oram

Altogether we spent 11 years in that flat and certainly the last few years there were far from pleasant. But it was while we were there that I began my book publishing career. In Belfast, I had become friendly with a publisher called John Murphy, who ran Appletree Press there and he invited me to edit my first book, on the unlikely subject of fishing in Ireland. The book came out in 1980 and since the text was written by three of the top fishing writers in Ireland, it got a good reaction and produced good sales. The next book, which came out in December, 1980, was entirely my own work, the history of the Bewley family and their cafés. That generated a lot of interest and goodwill and got off to a great start when Donal Foley gave it a great mention in The Irish Times.

Frankie Byrne, radio agony aunt, launched the book, even though she was far more nervous than anyone else at the reception in Hodges Figgis book shop in Dawson Street. One of the celebrated guests was the famous Dublin born actor, Noel Purcell. Then in 1983 came the first of my big books, the one on Irish newspaper history, published in 1983; the idea for that had come to Bernadette in a dream in bed one night.

All through the 1980s, I continued my job, a very tedious and boring one, editing magazines; I took no great enjoyment from it and the only compensation was that I

Bernadette and Hugh outside the old Cashel Palace
Hotel, Cashel, Co Tipperary, 1989.
Photo: Hugh Oram

was able to devote so much time to my fast developing book career. Then in the summer of 1988 and not before time, we had to move out of that flat, as the landlady wanted to sell it. We spent an absolutely frightful three months in a flat at the top of Ailesbury Road, a true hell on earth, while all the time we were looking for somewhere better. Then one day, on my walks around the district in search of somewhere pleasant to live, I spotted a vacant house in Wellington Lane, off Wellington Road. We did a deal and moved in on October 1, 1988.

The weekend before was hectic to say the least, as we went on a trip to Paris, leaving Dublin airport on the Friday evening on an Air France Concorde, an incredible experience. After the weekend in Paris, we returned to Dublin on the Sunday evening by Aer Lingus Boeing 737, which seemed like an old taxi after Concorde. The following day, we moved to our new house. It' s amazing to think that we' ve been there nearly 30 years now. We spent some weeks getting the place in order, so that we could invite Bernadette' s beloved parents over, but sadly, Hugh Quinn, her father, died in December, 1988, without ever seeing the house. Bernadette' s mother May saw the house once before she went into care.

The early to mid 1980s saw Bernadette' s poetry career come to an end; after her final poetry publication in 1986, she stopped writing. In 1989, I finally broke away from the frightful job in magazine publishing and became much more involved in the newspaper business. In 1991, when Bernadette was 61, we did our final trip outside Ireland, when we went to Strasbourg and Paris. By 1991, I had completed the mammoth job I had had since 1988 helping to research and write the Michelin Green Guide to Ireland. In the mid—1990s, I had a most enjoyable one day trip to Glasgow to do book research in the Mitchell Library, while I also had a most interesting and longer trip to London, at around the same time, again for book research.

Bernadette in Wicklow Town, with the Vartry River in the background.
Photo: Hugh Oram

During the 1970s and 1980s, we had done innumerable trips outside Ireland, some to Britain, but most to mainland Europe and one to Boston, that most Irish of all American cities. All our travels are documented in detail in my book, On Our Way, published in 2016. Bernadette was well able to cope with all the vagaries that travel brings and I always remember one auspicious occasion. We were flying from Paris to Strasbourg but no—one told the passengers until the flight was well under way that Strasbourg airport was closed for runway repairs and that the flight was being diverted to a military airfield about 50 km from Strasbourg.

When the plane landed, we found that no—one on the Air France staff had bothered to ask how the passengers were going to be transported to Strasbourg. All the other passengers, nearly all French, were standing around like a lot of bemused sheep. Bernadette took the bull by the horns, found some Air France ground staff and promptly berated them in fluent French for not organising transport to Strasbourg. Lo and behold, a short while later, a couple of coaches turned up and all the French passengers turned to Bernadette and with one voice, shouted in her direction: Jean d' Arc! It was a well—deserved compliment.

By the time the great economic crash came in 2008, I was well established in both the newspaper business and book publishing, but for a few years after that, it was often touch and go how we would survive, but survive we did. But sadly, over the past decade, Bernadette' s health continued to deteriorate, to the stage On October 8, 2016, she was admitted to St Vincent' s Hospital, Dublin. The social workers there told me that I couldn' t think in terms of bringing Bernadette home again, as she' s need so much care. So on November 29, 2016, she moved into St Mary' s Anglican home in Pembroke Park, just across the road from the house here. There, the care she has received has been so exemplary that her health has improved considerably and it' s a joy being able to go across the road and see her every day.

June, 2017 saw Bernadette and I married for 45 years, an epic voyage, and she has been a wonderful companion along the way, someone with a remarkable life story. Her sister Gloria, younger by five years, is also in a nursing home, off Newtownpark Avenue in Blackrock. Her wonderful husband, Eamonn Williams, died in 2005. But thankfully, Bernadette and I have been able to keep going such a strong bond for so many years, all the result of a chance meeting in the Department of Foreign Affairs 47 years ago.

Bernadette in Rouen cathedral, France,1990.
Photo: Hugh Oram

Bernadette on a bridge across the River Seine, Paris, 1990.On the right of the photograph is the Musée d´Orsay.
Photo: Hugh Oram